THE
HISTORICAL SOURCES OF DEFOE'S
JOURNAL OF THE PLAGUE YEAR

THE HISTORICAL SOURCES OF DEFOE'S JOURNAL OF THE PLAGUE YEAR

Illustrated

BY EXTRACTS FROM THE ORIGINAL DOCU-
MENTS IN THE BURNEY COLLECTION
AND MANUSCRIPT ROOM IN THE
BRITISH MUSEUM

By WATSON NICHOLSON, Ph.D.

KENNIKAT PRESS, INC./PORT WASHINGTON, N. Y.

THE HISTORICAL SOURCES OF DEFOE'S JOURNAL
OF THE PLAGUE YEAR

Originally published in 1920
Reissued in 1966 by Kennikat Press

Manufactured in the United States of America
Library of Congress Catalog Card No: 66-25934

PREFACE

At the outbreak of the Great War, and for some years prior to that world catastrophe, I was working in the British Museum, the Public Record Office, and the Lord Chamberlain's Office in London, pursuing certain investigations pertaining to the history of the English Drama and Stage. Throughout my quest among the documents of the years 1664 and 1665, I was again and again impressed with numerous striking resemblances between contemporaneous details of the Great Plague and Defoe's account in his *Journal of the Plague Year*. With a piqued curiosity I followed these clues until I had amassed overwhelming evidence of the complete authenticity of Defoe's "masterpiece of the imagination." These proofs were then submitted to a few scholars in England and America, and the unanimous and emphatic judgment of these critics was, that I had established beyond cavil the historical character of Defoe's famous *Journal,* hitherto not merely accepted, but acclaimed and declaimed, as fiction. However, to make assurance doubly sure, I pursued the investigation still further, and, in more than two hundred instances (not to mention the scores of statistical figures), recorded in the following pages, traced to their sources statements made by Defoe in the *Journal of the Plague Year.* In most cases the word-for-word originals have been quoted (or cited), and, added to these, equally convincing parallels have multiplied the proofs that Defoe relied upon facts in compiling his history of the Plague. So great is the mass of contemporaneous evidence leading to the conclusion arrived at in the course of this study that the bulk of the valuable data collected from the printed and unprinted sources has had to be omitted, both from the discussion and from the appendices, although a sufficient number of extracts have been included to establish fully the historical basis of every statement made by Defoe in the *Journal of the Plague Year*. The discovery and significance of the proofs herewith submitted were publicly accredited to me by Professor William Lyon Phelps in the *Bookman* (New York) for November, 1915.

W. N.

"Deer Lodge"
South Haven, Michigan
    July 4, 1919.

CONTENTS

CONTENTS

THE
HISTORICAL SOURCES OF DEFOE'S
JOURNAL OF THE PLAGUE YEAR

When a tradition once becomes established by the hallmark of acknowledged authority, it takes more than cold facts to uproot it from men's minds,—it takes time. Thus, from a careless statement, attributed to Sir Walter Scott, that Defoe's *Journal of the Plague Year* belongs to that "peculiar class of compositions which hovers between romance and history," others, wholly ignorant of the real facts, have enlarged upon the theme of the fictional element in the *Journal* until now it is innocently catalogued under "fiction" by reputable publishers. Even Sir Henry Ellis, in 1827, then Keeper of the MSS. in the British Museum, in a prefatory note to some letters concerning the Great Plague of 1665 (printed in *Original Letters*, 2nd Ser., Vol. IV), asserted, without qualification, that Defoe's *Journal* "was an entire fiction." This bald *dictum* often has been embroidered upon by unwitting editors, to the effect, for example, that the *Journal* is a masterpiece in its verisimilitude, and, although it presents many actual facts and figures, it is to be eschewed as a reliable reference on the Plague. Others have gotten so confused by their certainty, on the one hand, that the work is primarily one of the imagination, and, on the other, that it contains many probable facts, that the result falls little short of nonsense. For instance, Walter Wilson in his *Memoirs of Defoe* (1830, III, 510-13) informs us that "it would baffle the ingenuity of any but Defoe to

[1]

frame a history, of so many attributes, upon the basis of fiction.'' And Sir Walter Besant (Introduction to the *Journal,* Century Classics, p. xix) tells us that "that great physician, Dr. Mead, was so much deceived by the 'Journal' that he took it for an authentic document,'' and, immediately afterwards, that "no more authentic document could have been produced!'' Again, in the last edition of the *Dictionary of National Biography* (Art. "Defoe"), we read that Defoe's narrative "has an air of authority which imposed upon Dr. Mead . . . who quotes it as an authority.'' So, also, one of the latest editors of the *Journal* (ed. Everyman's Library, Introduction, p. ix) has a similar statement, viz., that it is "in some respects Defoe's masterpiece; and its realism, which is unsurpassed, caused Dr. Mead, the eminent physician of the time, to refer to the book some years afterwards as an authority;'' and the latest edition (11th) of *Encyclopaedia Britannica* (Art. "Plague") warns the reader that "Defoe's fascinating *Journal of a Citizen* should be read and admired as a fiction, but accepted with caution as history.''

There have been a few writers, indeed, heretical enough to break away from the ranks and assert that the *Journal* is legitimate history; but as these have merely asserted without proofs, their opinions are naturally passed over.[1] The general concensus is that Defoe creates a realistic atmosphere, and gives a cor-

[1] Thus Mr. Thomas Wright in his "Life of Defoe" (1894) iterates and reiterates (pp. 98, 230, 235, 294), "that the 'Journal' is veritable history, there is not the least doubt.'' In 1872, Mr. E. W. Brayley edited the "Journal" and supplied a great number of facts from contemporaneous sources relating to the Plague; but he made no attempt to establish Defoe's work as history.

rect impression of the Plague, but that he cannot be relied upon as an historian, that facts with him are but materials for his imagination, and that an artful style and inventive genius fix the *Journal* as a work of fiction rather than a narrative of historic facts. The foregoing quotations are sufficient evidence of the general belief. The simple truth is, however, there is not a single essential statement in the *Journal* not based on historic fact. Even the stories ascribed to Defoe's invention have their origins in real contemporaneous events. Indeed, one of Defoe's crowning achievements in compiling the *Journal* consisted in curbing his natural predilection for invention, and adhering to strict facts as he found them in printed sources or got them directly from the survivors of 1665. Defoe himself asserts (Introduction to *Due Preparations*)—and there is no sufficient reason to doubt him—that he well remembered the Great Plague. Defoe was about six in 1665, and, besides, he had a vast fund of dismal and graphic stories from the older survivors of the Plague. But here again the fiction theorist bolsters up his hypothesis with, ''The truth itself is not believed from one who often has deceived,'' and it is explained that Defoe warped and exaggerated actual conditions in order to heighten the effects of history. However, for one who has examined the sources of the *Journal*, it would be difficult, indeed, to conceive how the actual horrors of the Plague Year could be exaggerated. It is true there are slips and errors in the *Journal* (to be noted in another connexion), but scarcely one of these is essential to the correctness of the narrative as a whole, and they

[3]

are almost invariably due to misinformation or haste, and not to deliberate intention. This will more fully appear when it is understood that contemporaneous accounts of the Plague are not always in absolute accord in every detail, and that sometimes there are positive errors recorded. This fact explains most of Defoe's errors in the *Journal*. In general, he was scrupulously careful to avoid all appearances of misrepresentation. Indeed, in some instances where he warns us that he is not vouching for the truthfulness of a given statement, he is still quite in harmony with the facts. On the whole when we consider the short time Defoe must have given himself to fling his materials together—for so it was really done, and not as the result of a studied carelessness, as is sometimes supposed—the *Journal* is remarkably free from errors, and is, in the main, far more authentic than many another work that passes for history. In short, Defoe's chief purpose in the *Journal* was to give historic facts, and his deviations from actual facts are comparatively few and unimportant.

The failure of editors and commentators to recognize this truth, or, possibly their want of curiosity, has led them into strange absurdities. Following one another in the assumption that the *Journal* is mainly fiction, they have been compelled, like mediæval theologians, to bolster up their hypothesis by further assumptions. Thus, it is argued, there must have been an incentive and a motive, other than a desire to write history, in composing the *Journal*. Naturally, the incentive was a commercial one. And the motive? Well, in 1720, Marseilles was visited by a most devastating Plague which swept away nearly 100,000 of her inhabitants. London's terrible experience of 1665 was still fresh in the memories of many then living, and, to prepare her citizens against such another calamity, Defoe, forsooth, wrote a *fiction* entitled a *Journal of the Plague Year.* A mere statement of the theory proves its absurdity. Besides, the *Journal* did not appear for over a year after the Plague had ceased in Marseilles. Moreover, the public had been warned repeatedly by more than a score of volumes, beginning with Dr. Richard Mead's *Short Discourse Concerning Pestilential Contagion,* prepared as the result of a Royal Order, in 1720, as soon as the report of the Marseilles Plague reached England. Owing to Mead's contention that pestilence is a contagious disease, a perfect shower of controversial books and pamphlets on the subject was cast upon the public. That the intense interest aroused by the Marseilles Plague suggested the *Journal* there is not the slightest doubt, and it is no less certain that the motive suggested above for writing it is not the true one, for not only had that warning and preparation been given by others, admittedly more capable than Defoe for such a task, and that too in 1720, but also, Defoe would hardly have waited to publish a half-dozen other books before writing the *Journal* had he looked upon the latter as a humanitarian duty he was called upon to perform. Even his *Due Preparations for the Plague* could have had little direct relation to the Marseilles Plague, for the reason just stated, although it was avowedly written for the enlightenment of people of all classes, as to how to escape the distemper in case it should again visit England. The simplicity and directness of the latter book compared with the heterogeneous character of the *Journal* would also indicate the purpose of the *Due Preparations*. Aside from this consideration, it is very probable that the last-mentioned book was an aftermath of the *Journal* —common practice with Defoe—and also that it was intended to supply practical, simple advice to the people, in place of the confused, contradictory, and unintelligible muddle of directions that were foisted upon the public as a result of the controversy over Dr. Mead's book. If the *Journal* had been written with a similar motive, then all the statistics, relation of the progress of the distemper, most of the stories, descriptions of the appearance of the town, domestic and foreign trade, in fact everything in the book except those moralizing passages concerning the treatment and care of the diseased, in case the Plague should ever again visit England, would have been omitted and practical advice substituted. In other words, the materials and their treatment in the *Journal* are historical, those of *Due Preparations* admonitory. In fact, such advice as does appear in the *Journal,* given as if original with Defoe (hence lending a fictional tint to the narrative), is borrowed directly from his sources, Hodges, Kemp, Sydenham, Diemerbroeck, Mead, etc.

The mention of Dr. Mead makes it necessary to revert to the oft-quoted assertion that he was deceived by Defoe whom he quoted as authority on the Plague. The absurdity of this myth will appear at once when it is pointed out that, in the first place, Defoe and

Mead were contemporaries (Mead was born in 1673) and the latter would scarcely be taken in regarding events that happened so near his own time; and, secondly, Mead was himself an eminent specialist in pestilential diseases, and when he was appointed in 1720 (as already mentioned) to prepare a treatise to assist in warding off the Marseilles distemper, he made a searching study of the history of plague and of its treatment. That he should have been ignorant of the matters treated of by Defoe in the *Journal* is inconceivable. Nay, not only did he have a much broader knowledge of the subject than did Defoe, but instead of the latter furnishing him with facts concerning the Plague of 1665, the very reverse is true. One of the amusing things about it all is, that Mead's *Discourse Concerning the Plague* went through eight editions before Defoe's *Journal* appeared. It is hardly necessary to point out (except to future editors of the *Journal*) that Mead in none of these eight editions could have borrowed from the *Journal*. However, in 1744, Dr. Mead revised his book on the Plague, when he referred, on one page only (p. 106) to the *Journal*. This was in connection with the evil effects of shutting up victims of the distemper, a practice which led some in their delirium to break out of their prisons to seek refuge with their friends in the country, or build huts and tents for themselves in the open fields, or get on board ships in the river, or voluntarily shut themselves up in self-defence.

Now, assuming that all this were mere fiction (an assumption impossible from the nature of the disease and of humanity), it would not, in the first place, be such a tremendous feat of the imagination; and, secondly, seeing that it is but a single instance, one would hardly be justified in asserting that Dr. Mead had been very greatly taken in. The whole assumption, however, falls to the ground when it is known that every word of the passage in question is true, and common to the history of all plagues. Diemerbroeck (*de Peste,* p. 120, a copy of which Defoe possessed) asserts that he personally knew "that in many places the sick have chose to lay themselves in fields, in the open air, under the slightest coverings," rather than submit to the restraint and cruelties of nurses. Mead also quoted this passage in his eighth edition of the *Discourse* (p. xviii). In the last-mentioned work (p. xxxii) it is related that, during the Plague in Germany in 1712-13, three men shut up in Hamburgh escaped, took refuge in a barn in the country, where they were all found dead, when the barn and corpses were burned together. Incidentally, it may be mentioned that this case may have suggested to Defoe the story of the soldier, sailor, and joiner. That this was the manner in which the disease was scattered broadcast over the kingdom is supported by all the sources. Voluntary shutting up was also common, Dr. Burnett being a case in point (Pepys, *Diary* 11 June, 1665).

Thus far it would appear that Defoe was more indebted to Mead than the other way about,—and this takes no account of the treatment of the distemper. But it is not necessary even to suppose that Defoe was, in this instance, a borrower from Dr. Mead (although in *Due Preparations* we know that he did use the latter's work) : we may come nearer home for a genuine source. In *Newes* No. 83, there is a letter from Durham, dated 13 October, 1665, which reads as follows: "The contagion in this country, which was brought hither about three months since by certain passengers from London and Yarmouth, is now by the favour of God very much asswaged: Sunderland (to which place it was first of all brought) being now perfectly well, and the other infected places in a very hopeful condition. The sick persons are all of them removed out of town into huts built in the fields at a convenient distance for that purpose." To be sure, this does not quite satisfy the case, as here there is no suggestion of breaking out of shut up houses; but in the same "newsbook," No. 79, is a letter from Dorchester bearing date of 23 September, 1665, in which it was reported that a man escaped from London and "died within a mile of this town, after four days' sickness, and supposed to be of the Plague; but the hovell wherein he lay being boarded over and under, a pit was digged, and both hovel and corpse were buried together." One of the most striking proofs of Plague victims breaking out of shut-up houses and running into the country, occurs in a pamphlet entitled *The Shutting Up of Infected Houses,* etc. (1665), wherein it is asserted that sometimes those who are shut up break out and "run as far in City and country as our feet can carry us, . . . till at last we drop in some alley, field, or neighbour village." As this whole matter will be entered into fully elsewhere in this essay, it need only be remarked here that the evidence is abundant to establish from other sources every item in the passage in Mead's *Discourse* which is referred to the *Journal* as authority.

It is further to be observed that Defoe himself tells us in the *Journal* that "it is much to the satisfaction of me that write, . . . to be able to say that everything is set down with moderation, and rather within compass than beyond it"; and of the several stories he relates he asserts a very truth when he says that there are "divers parallel stories to be met with of the same kind." The force of this truth will more definitely appear in the course of this survey. In like manner, in *Due Preparations* (1722, Introduction, pp. x, xi) he assures us that his purpose is to keep near the facts, and, moreover, he informs us of his method. "To make this discourse familiar and agreeable to every reader," he says, "I have endeavoured to make it as historical as I could, and have therefore intermingled it with some accounts of fact, where I could come at them, and some by report, . . . The cases I have stated here, are suited with the utmost care to the circumstances past, and more especially as they are reasonably supposed to suit those to come; and as I very particularly remember the last visitation of this kind, which afflicted this nation in 1665, and have had occasion to converse with many other persons who lived in this city all the while, I have chosen some of their cases as precedents for our present instructions. I take leave so far to personate the particular persons in their histories, as is needful in the case in hand, without making use of their names, though in many cases I could have descended to the very names and particulars of the persons themselves." In these two quotations, the one from the *Journal*, the other from *Due Preparations*, we are presented with the true explanation of the purposes and methods in the two books respectively: both are based on authentic facts, in one case "set down with moderation, and rather within compass than beyond it," and in the other, "suited with the utmost care to the circumstances past, *and more especially as they are reasonably supposed to suit those to come.*" In other words, Defoe took two simple historic facts, the one of a man who saved himself and family by shutting themselves up before the Plague got into their neighbourhood, the other of a family who fled from the distemper, got aboard a ship, and thus escaped. Both of these instances appear in the *Journal*, intermingled with other incidents and episodes of the Plague Year. In *Due Preparations*, Defoe simply isolated these two common devices for escaping the Plague and, applying the method employed in *Robinson Crusoe*, elaborated and developed them into practical instructions. Due *Preparations* is thus much closer to fiction in method and style of narration than is the *Journal*, for only in one instance in the latter is there anything that approaches fiction, namely, the story of the soldier, sailor and joiner, and even here the several parts of the story are quite true; it is only the manner of combining them into a coherent narrative that suggests the fictional element. Other tricks of style and manner employed in the *Journal* that have deceived many into the belief that the materials themselves came out of Defoe's imagination, I shall discuss more fully in another section.

Turning to the second point in Defoe's Introduction to *Due Preparations*, viz., his "personation" of the characters he mentions therein, the same is true in a few cases in the *Journal*. Whenever the mention of an historic name would redound to the credit of the original, he did not scruple to use it. Thus, he enumerates four famous physicians who braved the perils of the Plague and remained in town to assist in administering to the poor stricken victims of the infection. These were Drs. Humphrey Brookes, Francis Upton, Nathaniel Hodges, and Peter Barwick, all honoured members of the College of Physicians, any one, or all, of whom Defoe may have known after he reached manhood.[2] On the other hand, when the mention of a particular historic character might cause offence,[3] or in any way interfere with his narrative, Defoe probably made up or borrowed a fictitious name; for it should not be forgotten that, as Defoe himself informs us, there were many yet alive in 1722 who could verify and parallel all, and many more, of his stories. And is it not a significant fact that in an age when every public statement was pounced upon

[2] Defoe might have mentioned many other brave physicians who offered themselves to the public service during the Plague, as Drs. Dey, Starkey, Grover, O'Dowd, Burnett, Davis, Thompson, D'Autry and Boghurst. The first five of these were martyrs to the distemper; Dr. William Boghurst recorded his very valuable observations in "Loimographia" (1666, but not printed until 1894 by the Epedemiological Society, ed. Dr. J. F. Payne); Dr. Geo. Thompson risked his life to dissect a Plague corpse, and recorded the experiment in "Loimotomia," 1666; Burnett was Pepys's doctor, and it was in his house in Fenchurch St. that the Plague first appeared in the City about the 10th of June. Ten weeks after his servant died of the Plague, Burnett himself succumbed to it. This illustrates the odd freaks of the disease mentioned by Defoe. Burnett was one of those who voluntarily shut himself up. See Pepys, "Diary," June 10, 11, Aug. 25, 1665.

[3] Strikingly exemplified in the case of the merchant who hanged himself in his delirium.

and mauled by every controversialist, no one, not even the survivors of 1665, seems to have doubted the authenticity of the *Journal?*[4] This matter of the fictitious names in Defoe's account of the Plague has been one of the sure evidences to commentators, of the fictitious nature of the *Journal*. Thus, they can find no Dr. Heath on record: *ergo,* he is a product of Defoe's genius. As a matter of very high probability, Dr. Heath was none other than Dr. Hodges, and, for the reasons given above, Defoe altered the name to Heath. In the hope of finding some clue to the name Heath, I sent for Goodall's *College of Physicians* (1684), a copy of which was in Defoe's library at the time of his death. I opened the book at random (p. 393) and by the strangest coincidence the first name my eye lighted upon was that of Sir Robert Heath (Lord Chief Justice under Charles I) standing out in capital letters to catch the eye. Much more to the purpose is the fact that the characteristics, including the discussions of the treatment of patients, etc., are applicable to Dr. Heath and Dr. Hodges alike. Also, when it is remembered that the latter is said to have suffered the same fate as the man Defoe mentions, who, following the doctor's instructions (identical with Hodges's prescription) to ward off the pestilence by a copious use of sack, got so addicted to the habit that he died a toper, we are able to appreciate the sentiment which moved Defoe to alter the name in the *Journal*. But this is a trivial matter which in no

[4] The continuator of Dr. Gideon Harvey's account of the Plague under the title of "City Remembrances" (1709) incorporated all the leading features of the "Journal," yet no one, I believe, has accused him of having been taken in.

sense detracts from the history as such. I take notice of it merely to cover the details of the *Journal*, and to indicate Defoe's probable motive in diverting his narrative from historic facts in matters likely to wound the feelings of those still alive when the *Journal* was written.

Another story that has aroused universal admiration of Defoe's genius is that of the Quaker, Solomon Eagle, who ran about the streets naked, predicting doleful things for London and crying, ''Oh the great and dreadful God!'' The only questions to be resolved, concerning this story, are, did people go about the streets naked, were Quakers particularly pessimistic in their prophecies, and was there a genuine historical character who might have furnished Defoe with a prototype? That people did go about naked we know from Thucydides, Vincent, and others; but they were usually frenzied victims of the pest. As for crepe-hanging prophets, they are common in all ages. Josephus's fanatic was one when he ran about wailing, ''Woe, woe to Jerusalem,'' before the destruction of that city by Titus. But we do not have to resort to ancient history or to generalities to account for Solomon Eagle. There was the flesh-and-blood John Gibson who might have done very well indeed for a model. He was a noted Quaker prognosticator of evil things, who lived during the middle of the 17th century, and, like Solomon Eagle, went about interpreting his ''visions,'' preaching his ''antient of dayes to come,'' and warning the people of Europe, ''but more particularly of England.''

[14]

More nearly parallel to the Solomon Eagle story are certain events of Defoe's own times. The history of the troublesome, prophesying Quakers of the 17th century and the early part of the 18th century is well known to students of the period, and Defoe especially had good cause to remember the dissenters of that time as one of his satirical pamphlets about them got him into serious trouble.[5] It may very well be that he had in mind one of these street-preaching prophets when he drew his Solomon Eagle. For example, on January 14, 1701, it is related that,

"This Day a Man Quaker came to the Royal-Exchange, about Exchange time, and took his Post by the Effigies of K. Charles 2. where the Spirit mov'd him to Express these Words; 'I am sent by the great God, to Proclaim his Summons to this great City; That in case the Inhabitants do not speedily Repent of their Wickedness, his Judgments will suddenly fall upon them.' "[6]

And again, a fortnight later, the following news item appeared in the same paper:

"London, Jan. 28, 1701. This day about 3 in the Afternoon, a Quaker Woman stept up upon a great Stone at Fleet-bridge, and made a speech there-

---

[5] "London, May 23, [1703]. Mr. Daniel de Foe, Author of The Shortest Way with the Dissenters, was taken on Thursday last [May 20] in a private House in Spittle-Fields."—"Daily Courant." May 24, 1703.
"London, July 31, [1703]. On the 29th Instant Daniel Foe, alias de Foe, stood in the Pillory before the Royal Exchange in Cornhill, as he did yesterday near the Conduit in Cheapside, and this day at Temple Bar, in pursuance of the Sentence given against him at the last Session of the Old-Bailey, for Writing and Publishing a Seditious Libel, Entituled, The Shortest Way with the Dissenters; By which Sentence he is also fined 200 Marks, to find Sureties for his good behaviour for 7 years, and to remain in Prison till all be performed."— "London Gazette," August 2, 1703.
[6] "London Post," January 15, 1700 (O. S.)

at, denouncing Woe to this City, if the Inhabitants do not speedily Repent.'"

I mention these few cases (which may be multiplied at will) to prove the abundance of the materials which Defoe might have drawn upon. That a genuine original supplied him with his Solomon Eagle is certain, and this is equally true of the story of the Whitechapel clergyman who went about repeating the liturgy.

Of a somewhat different nature is the circumstance related in the *Journal* of the blind piper, who, while overcome with drink, was picked up and thrown into the dead cart along with the corpses to be dumped into the pit. At first glance the whole thing is so bizarre that we are tempted to brand it as fiction of the grimmest sort. Yet a little industry rewards us with a genuine parallel. In William Austin's *Anatomy of the Pestilence in 1665* (p. 38), which, by the way, contains numerous other parallels to the *Journal*, we read in connection with the burial of the dead:

> Wisely they leave graves open to the dead
> 'Cause some too early there are brought to bed.
> . . . .
> One out of trance return'd, after much strife
> Among a troup of dead, exclaims for life.

Nor need the story related by Defoe of the demented man who thought he saw a ghost in Bishopsgate Churchyard cause great wonder or admiration. Any community in any age will supply many more fetching ghost stories than the one reproduced by Defoe. The

[7] "London Post," January 29, 1701.

subject was one that appealed to him, and his own library contained any number of examples, to say nothing of the wierd stories then, as always, current. Besides, hallucination is one of the leading symptoms of plague. George Withers, the poet, who won great distinction by remaining in London throughout the Plague of 1625 and also that of 1665, recorded his experiences and observations of the former in a large tome (in verse) entitled *Britain's Remembrancer*. In this there are literally dozens of parallel descriptions and stories to those in the *Journal,* and in this connection particularly a man who, in delirium, fancied he saw Death prowling about,

> . . . now by the bed,
> He stands, now at the foot, now at the Head.
> . . . .
> He acted with a look so tragical
> That all bystanders might have thought his eyes
> Saw real objects, and no fantasies.

Then there is the story in the *Journal* of the man who could detect the presence of an infected person by the smarting of a wound on his leg, when he would rise up, if in company, and say, "Friends, here is somebody in the room that has the plague," although there were no outward symptoms of it. This looks and sounds very much like invention on Defoe's part, but it is nothing of the kind, any more than the other stories in the *Journal* accredited to his genius. In a letter dated October 12, 1670, J. Beale wrote to the Hon. R. Boyle (*Works,* ed. 1772, VI, 429), that a person "whom for many years I have known to be creditable, [told me] that he knew a good old woman, aged near eighty, now deceased, who said often in his hearing, that she could know, if the plague were within thirty miles of her, by a pain she had in three plague sores, which sores she had in her younger days, before she was married." Certainly in this instance Defoe kept rather "within compass than beyond it." And here it should be observed that Defoe has been criticised for asserting that plague victims went about with the infection upon them, yet not be aware of it themselves "till they had the very tokens come out upon them, . . . and would die in an hour or two after they came home, but be well as long as they were abroad." This criticism (and, indeed, most of the criticism of the *Journal,* is based entirely on probability. An examination of the sources again justifies Defoe's claim to "moderation." On September 20, 1665, John Allin (preacher-chemist-astrologer), who remained in London throughout the Plague, wrote to his friend, Philip Fryth: "If the infection be received by the halitus, or breath, it now immediately afflicts the hearte, ye root of the vitall spirits, and some time kills before any external and generally believed symptomes of that distemper can appeare, either spotts or tumors, but allways invades ye party with sudden and sharpe fainting fitts."[8] Kemp gives testimony to the same effect when he quotes Benedictus as authority for the statement that plague victims sometimes "whilst they have been employed about their business in the house, their trading in the market, their devotions in

[8] "Archælogia," XXXVII, 12.

the church, have died suddenly, and sundry other physicians relate the like, and perhaps hath or might have been observed at London.''[9] The same author also gives his testimony that ''as the Plague is propagated by contagion, so likewise it is spread by fear and imagination. . . . There be stories that make the relation of some that did but see one infected with the Plague, and of some that did but behold afar off a corpse going to be buried; of others, who being in the house, did not hear the buriers, and presently after have sought the sickness, and died of the Plague themselves.''[10] Hodges, Vincent, and many others bear witness to this fact which recurs a number of times in the *Journal*.

The various stories of infected persons breaking out while insane from their sufferings, and often doing violence upon themselves or others, are all quite true and will be considered presently. The story of the waterman who was compelled to ply his vocation in order to earn a livelihood for his wife and child, though afraid to go near them for fear of carrying the distemper to them, and so deposited his earnings on a large stone where they might come out and get them, has the ring of reality about it. In like manner, Dr. Symon Patrick's clerk removed himself from his family, although in his case he did it to protect himself from those of his household who were visited.[11] It is only in the story of the three friends who escaped into the country and lived in a tent that Defoe abandons himself to the methods of fiction; but,

[9] Kemp. ''Brief Treatise,'' p. 3.
[10] Ib. p. 22.
[11] Add. MSS., 5810.

as already pointed out, all the details of the story essential to the history of the Plague are in accord with known facts: people did escape and live in tents and huts, and the country folk were chary of them.

The feature of the history of the Plague relating to the breaking out of victims from shut-up houses, and in some cases the escape of people before their houses were shut up, they running into the country with the infection upon them, thus polluting places hitherto free from the contagion, occupies a most important place in the *Journal,* involving at least one-seventh of its entire contents, albeit there are many useless repetitions. The arguments for and against shutting up were taken by Defoe directly from Hodges's "Historical Account of the Plague of 1665;" and other sources are numerous. So, also, the stories repeated by Defoe to illustrate the plain facts have numerous origins and parallels. Some of these have already been mentioned in other connections. The author of *Shutting Up Infected Houses as it is practised in England* (1665) gives us an appalling account of the evils arising from shutting up. "As soon as we find ourselves or any member of our families infected," he says, "so dreadful is it to us to be shut up from all comfort and society, from free and wholesome air, from the care of the physician and divine, from the oversight of friends and relations, and sometimes from the very necessities and conveniences of nature, that we run as far in city and country as our feet can carry us, leaving wives and children to the parishes, empty walls and shops to creditors, scattering the infection along the streets as we go, and shifting it from lodging to lodging with ourselves, till at last we drop in some alley, field or neighbour village, calling the people round about by the suddenness of our fall to stand awhile astonished at our deaths, and then take their own; each fearful man of us frighted from his own house, killing his own town by surprising them unprepared. . . .

"See, see, we infect not our next neighbours, and this sickness spreads not much in any one place, but we carry it from place to place, running from our homes as from places of torment, and thus the roads are visited, and men travel the same way to the country, and to their long home. Thus the contagion hath reached most places round the city, which is now as it were besieged with the judgment, and encompassed with the visitation and desolation." And the author of *Golgotha* (p. 12) says of the evil of shutting up that "many for fear thereof do hide their sores, and, after a sweat or two, their sickness also, and go daily about their business as long as they can stand, mingled to much more danger every way. Nor dare any do the office of a nurse or friend to those shut up . . . because it is so penal that they must be inclosed then themselves."

It was in the manner of the foregoing examples that Islington received the infection, as related by Defoe in the story of the man who died at the "Pied Bull." Leafing over the "newsbooks" of 1665, we find any number of similar stories. To take one instance, in a letter from Portsmouth, dated September 3, 1665, we are informed that the Plague had got over to Newport—isolated as that town was—

"brought over by a certain knight who had an estate there, and sickened and died at his lodgings; the master of the house thought it quinsy, and threatened the mayor for shutting up the house, but two women took the infection, and died from merely changing and airing the sheets of the bed; the poor gentleman was obliged to bury the bodies himself in his own garden; sheep and goats since put in the house are all dead." Again, in a letter from Coventry, October 15, 1665, we read: "We were very much afraid of the sickness at Litchfield, and it is true that a disorderly fellow entertained an infected person in an ale-house in the suburbs: whereupon the master of the house died." In Defoe's story it was the maid who showed the traveler to his room who "fell presently ill." But the resemblances between all these stories are so unmistakable that historical accuracy is assured. Well might the country places be suspicious of people from London!

At the outbreak of the Plague, as related by the contemporaries, and repeated by Defoe, only, or mainly, those who were financially able to run away from the distemper left town; but as the enormity of the disease became more and more apparent, those who had at first hesitated to go, got away whenever possible. By this time the Plague was approaching its height, and hence travelers from London were the more feared. The country magistrates were put to their wits' ends to prevent strangers entering their precincts. Commercial interests, however, and forged certificates of health made it possible for many to go from place to place; and the mere desperation of shut-up victims, as related by the author of *Shutting up,* made it impossible to guard successfully against the ultimate spread of the disease. Nevertheless, the whole country was so alarmed, the vigilance of the authorities so alert, that a fairly rigid quarantine was established in most places until after the Plague approached its climax in London. The experience of Defoe's three heroes is typical of what happened to most travelers during that frightful year. By the end of June, 1665, every one knew that the Plague was rapidly getting beyond control, and those who were able to do so had left town or were preparing to leave. Pepys's entry for June 29 depicts the situation very tersely: "Up and by water to White Hall, where the Court full of waggons and people ready to go out of towne. . . . This end of the towne grows every day very bad of the plague. The Mortality Bill has come to 267." The "great orbs," as Vincent calls the aristocracy, went first of course,—many even long before the Court fled, for it was not until July 2 that Charles II and his retinue went to Hampton Court (the Queen Mother left for France on June 26); but the general exodus had begun before the middle of June, and a few had taken the alarm and gone when the Bills ending June 6 showed an increase from 17 to 43 of the Plague; and when, the following week, 112 deaths from the distemper were reported, the real panic began, as recorded by Defoe. This was reflected the following day (June 14) when a royal Proclamation was issued forbidding the holding of the annual Fair at Barnwell, near Cambridge,—the first of many similar prohibitions. The country towns at once began to erect barriers against travelers from the metropolis: a clean bill of health was required of all strangers, especially from London, but, as already observed, this means of protection had to be abandoned soon for more drastic methods.[12] Among the first towns to take due precautions was (by the irony of fate, as it was later most heavily visited) Ipswich. On July 11, 1665, its correspondent to the *Newes* (No. 54) reported that the place was in good health, "and there is great care and industry used to keep it so, no stranger being permitted to enter without examinations and good Certificates." The officials of Ipswich did not then know how easy it was to secure "good Certificates."

The precautions taken by the Guildford authorities are worth repeating as they are fairly representative of the action taken by most of the country towns to prevent the Plague from visiting them: "As it hath pleased God hitherto to preserve this place and the neighbourhood in a happy condition of health; so it is the singular care of the magistrates to provide (as much as may be) for the continuance thereof; to which end Justices of the Peace of County of Surrey have directed an Order of Sessions, bearing date the 11th, instant, [July, 1665], to the lord of the Manor of Ebisham, desiring him to cause the wells to be locked up

---

[12] "Whereas several Certificates have been made by others as from the Officers of St. Gregory's Parish by St. Paul's, London: This is to notify that the Officers of the said Parish will not certify any to be clear of the Plague but whom they know, and that from the 8th of this instant [July 1665], they will subscribe to no Certificates but what are printed."—"Intelligencer," No. 53—There are many other advertisements like this one, and they all clearly indicate that forged certificates were common. Unfortunately, the deceit was not discovered in time, and it may easily be understood how suspicious the magistrates became, even of those bearing certificates. The story of Defoe's three heroes should be read in this light.

during these infectious times, and to secure the same by a constant watch, for fear of any resort thither from infectious places: which said Order was upon Monday last put into execution, with a restraint upon the inhabitants, neither to receive any lodgers into their houses, nor to admit any coaches or waggons with goods or passengers from infected places. Which Order was not resolved upon without great reluctancy, considering the damages of particulars which must necessarily attend it.''[18] Vincent, in *God's Terrible Voice in the City,* calls attention to the quarantine established in the country towns: ''Now the countries [*i. e.* country towns] keep guards, lest infectious persons from the City bring the disease unto them;'' and the Sancroft Correspondence (November 2, 1665) speaks of the ''unkindnesse of country people to Londoners.'' On July 17, Pepys comments, ''Lord! to see how all these great people here [at Dagnams, near Romford] are afeard of London, being doubtful of anything that comes from thence, or that has lately been there, that I was forced to say that I lived wholly at Woolwich.'' On September 3, he was obliged to go to Greenwich on business connected with the Admiralty, ''where much ado to be suffered to come into the towne, till I told them who I was.'' A week earlier he recorded that it was ''an unpleasing thing to be at Court [then at Hampton Court], everybody being fearful one of another, and all so sad, enquiring after the Plague.''

In an effort to assist the country towns to make their restrictions more effective, the King on August

[18] ''Intelligencer,'' No. 57.

10, 1665, sent a command to the Middlesex Justices to use diligence in preventing the removal of persons or goods from London and suburbs to other towns; and likewise to suppress the practice of infected persons breaking out of shut-up houses. Searchers, nurses, etc., were to be appointed in the towns in the Magistrates' jurisdiction, and no lodger or tenant was to be admitted without the permission of two Justices of the Peace. The part played by high Church officials in preventing the spread of the distemper is also worthy of note. Thus, to mention only one example, the Bishop of Ely temporarily nullified the patent for holding the annual Fair at Ely, for fear of "a great resort from London, Yarmouth, Colchester, Cambridge, and other places."[14]

Despite all efforts to prevent the spread of the disease (in London by means of shutting up infected houses, in the country by orders regulating travel and traffic), the Plague finally got to almost every part of England.[15] Defoe has faithfully recorded how this came about, namely, by infected persons bribing the watchmen or otherwise escaping from shut-up houses, and by others getting away before the infection was discovered upon them, and before their houses were shut up. Defoe's three travelers were free from the distemper, it is true; but the reverse was as apt to be the case. Pepys (*Diary*, September 3, 1665) gives us

[14] "Intelligencer," No. 78.
[15] Scotland, which had been visited in a most frightful manner in former plague years, forbade (July 12, 1665) all persons from England to enter her borders, on penalty of the loss of life and goods, unless "they bring sufficient passes and testimonials with them, under the hands and seals of the Major and Aldermen." "Newes," No. 58. No wonder Defoe remarked that he did not know "how it fared with Scotland,"— there was no plague news from Scotland.

a graphic picture of an evasion of the shutting up and guarding order. "Among other stories," he says, "one was very passionate, methought, of a complaint brought against a man in the towne [of Greenwich] for taking a child from London from an infected house. Alderman Hooker told me it was the child of a very able citizen in Gracious Street, a saddler, who had buried all the rest of his children of the plague, and himself and wife now being shut up, and in despair of escaping, did desire only to save the life of this little child; and so prevailed to have it received stark-naked into the arms of a friend, who brought it (having put it into new fresh clothes) to Greenwich; whereupon hearing the story, we did agree it should be permitted to be received and left in the towne."

The frenzy of shut-up victims, when the fever was at its height, causing them to do violence upon themselves or others, made a strong appeal to Defoe, as to all students of the Plague. One thus crazed, mentioned in the *Journal*, broke out of his bed, ran naked through the streets to the Thames, plunged in, swam across and back, and was soon after a well man. Thucydides likewise records that those visited with the distemper could not endure clothing upon them, and that nothing pleased them so much as to plunge into water. Add to this statement of Thucydides the debate over the cold water cure, and we have Defoe's story; and note here too, as so often in the *Journal*, its author does not vouch for the truthfulness of the story. Another instance of a similar nature is of one who, "in or about Whitecross Street burned himself to death in his bed." As this was taken directly from

Vincent's *God's Terrible Voice in the City* (which also furnished numerous other facts for the *Journal*), it was not necessary to warn the reader that it might not be authentic,—Defoe got it from undoubted authority. Of violence upon others, when the infected were delirious, examples are only too numerous. The author of *Shutting up Infected Houses* relates that in their paroxysms of pain the sick "are ready to commit any violence, either upon themselves or others, whether wife, mother, or child," and, by the method adopted by Defoe, cites a specific example "last week in Fleet Lane, where the man of the house being sick, and having a great swelling, . . . did in a strong fit rise out of his bed, in spight of all that his wife (who attended him) could do to the contrary, got his knife and most miserably cut his wife, and had killed her, had she not wrapped up the sheet about her, and therewith saved herself, till by crying out Murther, a neighbour . . . came seasonably to her preservation. The man is since dead."

Of the mournful stories and descriptions in the *Journal*, one enthusiastic editor exclaims in admiration, "Nothing could be more tragic," etc.,—as if Defoe's imagination were the author of the tragedy! A few brief glances through the account just quoted from, or at the pages of Withers, Austin, Hodges, Vincent, and others, would reveal not only more tragical scenes, but more pathetic and more graphic, than those in the *Journal*. Take, for example, this vivid description of the horrors of the Plague:[16]

[16] George Withers, "Britain's Remembrancer," fol. 105. That this refers to the Plague of 1625 makes nothing against it as evidence,— the histories of all plagues are filled with identical

Here, one man stagger'd by with visage pale;
There, lean'd another grunting on a stall;
A third, half dead, lay gasping for his grave;
A fourth did out of window call and rave;
Yon, came the bearers sweating from the Pit,
To fetch more bodies to replenish it.
A little further off, one sits and shows
The spots, which he death's tokens doth suppose;

. . . .

       Yea, the terror
Occasioned by their fond and common error,
Who tell the sick that markt for death they be,
(When those blue spots upon their flesh they see)
Even that hath murthered thousands who might here
Have lived, else, among us, many a year.

And there is nothing in Defoe's narrative that for an instant can be compared with the following extract from *God's Terrible Voice*: "In August ... the people fell as thick as leaves from the trees in Autumn, ... and there is a dismal solitude in London streets. ... Now shops are shut in, people rare and very few that walk about, insomuch that grass begins to spring up in some places, especially within the Walls; no rattling coaches, no prancing horses, no calling in customers, no offering wares, no London cries sounding in the ears; if any voice be heard it is the groans of dying

horrors. It will be observed that Withers speaks of people dying of fright; practically all the sources agree on this point,— Hodges, Vincent, Kemp, "J. V.," Boghurst, etc. On August 9, 1665, Pepys wrote in his "Diary": "An odd story of Alderman Bunce's stumbling over a dead corpse in the streets, and going home and telling his wife, she at the fright, being with child, fell sick and died of the plague." Defoe had ample authority for a similar story.

persons breathing forth their last; and the funeral knells of them that are ready to be carried to their graves. Now shutting up of visited houses, there being so many, is at an end, and most of the well are mingled among the sick, which otherwise would have got no help. Now in some places where the people did generally stay, not one house in an hundred but is infected, and in many houses half the family is swept away,—in some the whole. . . . Now the nights are too short to bury the dead, the whole day (though at so great a length) is hardly sufficient to light the dead that fall therein into their beds.

"Now, we could hardly go forth, but we should meet many coffins, and see many with sores and limping in the streets; amongst other sad spectacles, methought two were very affecting: one of a woman coming alone and weeping by the door where I lived (which was in the midst of the infection) with a little coffin under her arm, carrying it to the new churchyard. I did judge it was the mother of the child, and that all the family besides was dead, and she was forced to coffin up and bury with her own hands this her last dead child." The other story related by Vincent is that of a plague victim who was seized with a fit near the Artillery Wall against which he dashed his head, "and when I came by he lay hanging with his bloody face over the rails, and bleeding upon the ground. As I came back he was removed under a tree in Moore-fields and lay upon his back; I went and spake to him; he could make me no answer, but rattled in his throat, and, as I was informed, within half an hour died in the place." It will be necessary to

[30]

mention Vincent again, but from this brief quotation it will at once be apparent that not only did Defoe borrow from him liberally of material and style (*cf.* whole families and whole streets swept away, grass growing in the streets, sad sights of victims limping about, etc.), but also how far short the later writer fell in emulating his source. There is nothing in the *Journal* that approaches the delineations of the genuine eye-witness, as to tragic pathos and graphic portrayal. Even the very exclamations of compassion, intended by Defoe to arouse pity, are taken directly over by him from the sources, which supplied him with his materials also. Not only so, but these exclamations occur invariably in the exact connections where they appear in the originals. Thus, "it would wound the soul of any Christian to have heard" the penitent groans of sinners—which occurs three times in the *Journal*—was borrowed from Vincent (*op. cit.* p. 25). So, also, "it often pierced my very soul to hear the groans and cries," "it was indeed a lamentable thing to hear the lamentations of poor dying creatures," or, "it would make the stoutest heart bleed to hear," etc., or, "it would make the hardest heart move," etc., or, "it was enough to place horror on the stoutest heart in the world," are no more a part of Defoe's lauded piety than are the other mythical attributes with which he has been invested by vapouring admirers. These are nothing but paraphrases of the common pious expressions of contemporaneous writers on the Plague. Compare, for example, one of Defoe's main sources, Hodges's *Loimologia*: "Who can express the calamities of such times !

The whole British Nation wept." Again, "Who would not burst with grief," etc., or, "even the relation of this calamity melts me into tears." George Withers (*op. cit*, 70) has a like expiration in,

> Ah me! what tongue can tell the many woes,
> What mortal pen is able to express, etc.

And Evelyn, who like Withers remained in London during the Plague of 1665, exclaims, "My very heart turns within me at the contemplation of our calamity."[17] To take still another example, on September 14, 1665, J. Tillison wrote to Dean Sancroft, "y^t heart is either steel or stone y^t will not lament for this sad visitation, & will not bleed for these vnutterable sorrowes;" and again in the same epistle, "What ey: would not weep," etc. That the last two quotations could not have been known to Defoe only serves to emphasize his unoriginality in his expression of a pious horror: such expressions were the fashion of the time. And the same may be said of the religious element which crops out here and there in the *Journal*, its expression was borrowed along with the rest. To take a case in point, his "divine meditations" and his sermon on blasphemy may have been suggested by or supplied from, any number of sources, as Withers's *Britain's Remembrancer*, Patrick's *An Exhortation*, etc., or the latter's numerous meditations and sermons which were very popular in Defoe's time (more than one hundred of them being in print in 1722, several of which Defoe had in his own library), and Vin-

[17] "Memoirs and Correspondence," ed. 1818, II, 212.

cent's *God's Terrible Voice* and, particularly, his sermon preached on the occasion of the funeral of Abraham Janaway, Sept. 18, 1665. Not even the oft-repeated "dismal objects," "dismal scenes," "dismal time," etc., are original with Defoe, but are copied by him from Vincent's "dismal solitude," Hodges's "dismal prospect," etc. Defoe's "Scarce a day or night passed over but some dismal thing or other happened," appears in Vincent as, "Scarcely a day passed over my head for I think a month or more together, but I should hear the death of some one or more that I knew." In both cases, the expressions follow immediately after the story of the man who burnt himself to death in bed. The little mannerisms, "I say," "As I said before," "If I may give my opinion," etc. are likewise reflections from the originals. "I say," was a particular favourite with Boccaccio (*cf.* 1st Day of *Decameron*). Indeed, the resemblance between Defoe's expressions and those of his sources are so marked as to lead to the conclusion that not only did he copy facts, but also the very language, from the originals. Even his opinions respecting the care and treatment of the plague-seized, the prevention of the disease spreading, questions of quarantine, public fires, fumigation, etc., so generously made a part of Defoe's originality by commentators, are borrowed from his sources. Thus, the argument for the spread of the distemper by contagion came from Hodges and his followers, as did the *pro* and *con* discussions of shutting up, the efficacy of fires in the streets, etc. The numerous medical treatises on the distemper from Diemerbroeck to Mead and Quincy furnished Defoe materials of that nature.

In a few instances, Defoe parts, or partially parts, company from his sources. An example of this is the case of wicked nurses. Almost without an exception the authorities who mention the subject agree that nurses often hastened the death of their patients by poisoning, smothering, or otherwise bringing about their end, with the purpose of robbing the dead. Defoe, true to his task, repeats their evidence, but doubts there was "more of tale than truth in those things." While his dissent is purely gratuitous, it in no sense confuses the record of fact. The stories of robberies alleged to have been committed by the nurses, after the members of a plague-stricken family were all dead, even to the taking of the linen from the bed and the clothes from the corpses, he accepts without question, but, oddly enough, similar stories related of the buriers he "cannot easily credit anything so vile among Christians." Nevertheless, he relates the stories,—the main thing so far as history is concerned. Both as regards the wicked nurses and the dishonest buriers there is abundant of evidence, though, naturally, more against the criminal nurses, as they had the first opportunity to rob the dead. On this point, Dr. Hodges's testimony is beyond dispute. "These wretches, out of greediness to plunder the dead," he says (*Loimologia,* ed. 1720, p. 8) "would strangle their patients, and charge it to the distemper in their throats; others would secretly convey the pestilential taint from sores of the infected to those who were well; and nothing indeed deterred these abandoned

[34]

miscreants from prosecuting their avaricious purposes by all the methods their wickedness could invent. . . . One amongst many, as she was leaving the house of a family, all dead, loaded with her robberies, fell down dead under her burden in the streets. And the case of a worthy citizen was very remarkable, who being suspected dying by his nurse, was beforehand stripped by her; but recovering again, he came a second time into the world naked.'' Austin corroborates all this in his *Anatomy of the Pestilence* (1665):

He'll [*i. e.* the patient] ne'er give out she killed him,
    for 'tis said,
He's to be always silent when he's dead.
And while he lives, nurses he'll never curse,
Knowing few good, most bad, and many worse.

That many searchers were dishonest, we learn from the same historian, who likewise furnishes us with further evidence that some were robbed before they were dead, and of the winding sheet afterwards.

Those there [at the grave] we thought bid us their last
    adieu,
Before they can repent are born anew.
They, walking, speak, thinking they may be bold,
Wanting their clothes, to say they are a-cold.

And again, with fine irony,

  One too too weak to raise his aking head,
  Throws off the sheet when friends have sold his bed.

And so on, in half-a-dozen similar examples.

Vincent supports this testimony when he says that, after the order for shutting up of houses had been issued, and the inscription, *Lord have mercy upon us,* set over the door, none was suffered to come to the pent-up victims "but a nurse, whom they have been more afraid of than the Plague itself."

But it is the vitriolic pen of the author of *Shutting up Infected Houses* that depicts the nurses of 1665 in the blackest shade. "Little is it conceived," he writes, "how careless most nurses are in attending the visited, and how careful (being possessed with rooking avarice) they are to watch their opportunity to ransack their houses; the assured absence of friends making the sick desperate on the one hand, and them on the other unfaithful: their estates are the Plague most die on, if they have anything to lose, to be sure those sad creatures (for the nurses in such cases are the off-scouring of the City) have a dose to give them; besides that it is something beyond a Plague to an ingenious spirit to be in the hands of those dirty, ugly, and unwholesome hags; even a hell itself, on the one hand to hear nothing but screetches, cries, groans, and on the other to see nothing but ugliness and deformity, black as night, and dark as Melancholy: Ah! to lie at the mercy of a strange woman is sad; to leave wife, children, plate, jewels, to the ingenuity of poverty is worse; but who can express the misery of being exposed to their rapine that have nothing of the woman left but shape?"[18]

---

[18] One of the stories (essentials taken from Hodges) which Defoe relates is of a nurse who smothered a victim by "laying a wet double clout" on his face. The language adopted in telling this seems to have been suggested by the 2nd Book of Kings, viii, 15: "And it came to pass on the morrow, that he took a thick

Another minor divergence between Defoe and his sources is found in the question of the alleged pleasure, or at least gross carelessness, which infected persons manifested in consciously infecting others. But here again, all the authorities are against him. Defoe repeats the assertion (with his denial) a number of times in the *Journal,* and also gives arguments (taken straight from Hodges's *Loimologia,* p. 10, and Mead's *Short Discourse,* 8th ed., p. xvii) for this cruel perversity of human nature. In support of the fact, as related in the works mentioned, we read in Pepys's *Diary* for February 12, 1666: "Comes Mr. Cæsar, my boy's lute-master, whom I have not seen since the plague before. . . . He tells me in the height of it, how bold people there were, to go in sport to one another's burials; and in spite too, ill people would breathe in the face . . . of well people." On August 22, 1665, he laments that the Plague "makes us more cruel to one another than if we are doggs;" and again to the same effect on September 4 following. Defoe's own faithful record (corroborated by Pepys, the "newsbooks" and others) that people persisted in crowding to burials, and so spread the infection, should have corrected his "opinion" to a large degree, for such gatherings were due to sheer morbidity and a dogged perversity.[19] But here, once more, we are

cloth and dipped it in water, and spread it on his face, so that he died." The practice of smothering was a common one, by report, in 1665.

In most of the quotations which I have given to illustrate a single point, other parallels to the "Journal" will at once suggest themselves.

[19] In "Newes" No. 71 (August 29, 1665), L'Estrange thus complains: "The late encrease of the sickness in and about this town (beside that the Judgement is in itself just and dreadful) has been undoubtedly promoted by the incorrigible license of the multitudes that resort to publick funerals, contrary both

supplied with the historical account and are distinctly told that the narrator is merely expressing an opinion,—a legitimate license practised by all historians, some of whom, indeed, unlike Defoe, often substitute opinion for fact. It is Defoe's very frankness which has caused him to be suspect.

Another point on which Defoe numerously expresses an opinion is in regard to the inaccuracies of the Bills of Mortality, as officially reported every week. In this he is only following the unanimous judgment of contemporary authorities. Thus, Hodges (*op. cit.*, 28) gives the estimated total of deaths from the Plague in 1665 as being over 100,000 (the Bills reported only 68,596). Defoe accepts Hodges's estimate (without naming the authority) as low enough. Also, like Hodges, Boghurst, and others, he points out the probability that victims of the Plague were often reported as having died of other diseases. Commenting on the discrepancies in the returns by the Parish Clerks, the author of *Reflections on the Weekly Bills of Mortality* (1665) observes that "there lyeth an error in the accounts or distinctions of casualities, that is, more died of the Plague than were accounted for under that name, as many as one to four, there being a fourth part more dead of other casualities in Plague years than the years preceding

to order and reason." And Pepys "Diary," September 3, 1665: "Lord! to consider the madness of the people of the town, who will (because they are forbid) come in crowds along with the dead corpses to see them buried." Again, three days later, he "saw in broad daylight two or three burials upon the Bankside, one at the very heels of another; and yet forty or fifty going along with every one of them." It will be remembered, also, that Pepys, just as Defoe's sadler, could not resist the temptation to prowl about to see how the Plague was progressing, even to going to burials. Cf. "Diary," August 30, 1665.

or subsequent: whence we may collect a good rule, *viz.* That whereas it is doubted we have not a true account of the number that died . . . of the Plague, the poor searchers, out of ignorance, respect, love of money, or malice, returning, it's suspected, more or less as they are inclined; we may discern the truth, by comparing the number that died of other diseases, and the casualities the weeks immediately before the Plague begun, and the numbers reported to have been dead every week of those diseases and casualities since, and observing that the surplusage that die now above what did then of those diseases, are indeed dead of the Plague, though returned under the notion of those other diseases." Writing on August 24, 1665, John Allin (*Archaelogia*, xxxvii, 6) reported 4,257 dead of the Plague for that week, "but rather in verity 5,000, though not so many in yᵉ bill of the Plague." This estimated discrepancy is less than that of John Graunt's, just quoted. On the other hand, Clarendon (*Continuation of the Life of*), with his usual inaccuracy avers that the Bills returned "above one hundred and three score thousand persons: and many who could compute very well concluded that there were in truth double that number who died; and that in one week, when the Bill mentioned only six thousand, there had in truth over fourteen thousand died." It may be stated, not in support of these exaggerations, but as a matter of contemporaneous opinion, that as many as eight thousand or ten thousand died in one week in September, when the Plague was at its height.[20] Of far greater value in Clarendon's account are the ex-

[20] See "Loimologia," 16; Pepys, August 31, 1665; Evelyn, September 7, 1665.

planations he gives for the misrepresentations in the
Bills. "The frequent deaths of the Clerks and Sextons of Parishes," he continues, "hindered the exact
account of every week; but that which left it without
any certainty was the vast number that was buried in
the fields, of which no account was kept. Then of the
Anabaptists and other sectaries who abounded in the
City, very few left their habitations; and multitudes
of them died, whereof no church-warden or other of-
ficer had notice; but they found burials according to
their own fancies, in their own gardens or the next
fields." Of this class, though not mentioned by
Clarendon, were the Quakers, who refused to have the
bell rung for their dead whom they buried without
making report of the fact to the Parish Clerk.[21]   It is
also pretty evident that the authorities "doctored"
the Bills before they were published. As an example
of this, Pepys records a detail in point (*Dairy*, August
30, 1665): "Up betimes . . . and abroad and met with
Hadley, our clerke, who, upon my asking how the
plague goes, he told me it encreases much, and much in
our parish [St. Olave, Hart St.]; for, says he, there
died nine this week, though I have returned but six:
which is a very ill practice, and makes me think it is
so in other places, and therefore the plague much
greater than people take it to be." More particularly
in a letter dated December 5, 1665, from Dr. Symon
Patrick to Mrs. Elizabeth Gauden, we are told that
"the just number [of dead] they [*i. e.* the clerks]

---

[21] On September 14, 1665, J. Tillison wrote to Dean Sancroft: "The
Quakers (as we are informed) have buryed in their peece 1000
for some weekes together last past, . . . & many other places
about ye town are not included in ye bill of Mortality." Cf.
Pepys, August 31, 1665.

would not declare, because the Lord Mayor must have it first: I heard lately that he imprisoned one of the officers because they spread abroad the account before they came to him: which indeed was unhandsome."[22] Once again, Defoe recorded the facts "within compass."

The great fascination of the *Journal* is not in the isolated stories used to illustrate a given phase or stage of the Plague—such as those I have dealt with thus far —but more particularly in the constant impressing upon the reader the general desolation of the town,— empty streets with grass growing therein, lack of trade, shut-up shops, doleful appearance of the people one met with, some full of sores, and all afraid of one another, the rumbling of the dead cart, the bell always tolling, and the ever ceaseless "Bring out your dead!" dinging mortality into the very soul. Of such instances, the duplicate sources are so numerous that only a few may be mentioned here. Hodges, Vincent, and other originals who certainly supplied Defoe with the bulk of his materials which he used to illustrate the pathetic side of the Plague, I shall reserve for another place, and reproduce here only extracts from parallel sources, some of which Defoe could have known nothing. As people began thoroughly to realize the horrors of the distemper, Austin (*Anatomy*, p. 8, *et sq.*) describes them,

So timorously they talk, look pale, and stare,
As if they had been frighted by the air.

[22] Add. MSS., 5,810.

The same historian records that the Inns of Court were closed, shops were shut up, and the Court left town,—

> The only thriving trade one can tell here
> Lives by the dead (as hangmen),— coffin-seller;
> .   .   .   .
> At ev'ry door stand marshall'd in array
> Biers, as green boughs are planted there in May.

People kept to the middle of the street, the sight of an infected house aroused horror, the town was so forlorn that,

> Did Cæsar now enter our City gate,
> His prize would make him think h'had found
>   a cheat.

> Of the great pit and the numerous burials,

> Many attend them to the graves are taught
> How to come there next day; so then are brought.
> .   .   .   .
> In this, the grave's great Jubilee, we choose
> No place but church-yard for our rendezvous.

The awful carnage, the pest stalking about everywhere —in the market, in the bread sent to preserve life, on the breath of a friend or relative, in the very letter wishing "long life and perfect health;"

> And to speak our condition at the best,
> Our City's merely but great house of pest.

Withers depicts similar scenes and conditions, and many more, too long and too numerous to quote.

> Death lurk't at ev'ry angle of the street,

And,

> In sundry families there was not one
> Whom his rude hand did take compassion on:
> Nay, many times he did not spare the last,
> Until the burial of the first was past.[23]

Turning to the Sancroft Correspondence (*Harleian MSS.* 5784-5), of which Defoe could have known nothing, in a letter from J. Tillison to Dean Sancroft, bearing date September 14, 1665, we read even a more pathetic tale of sorrow and desolation: "What ey: would not weep to see soe many habitacons vninhabited? ye poore sick not visited? ye hungry not fed? ye grave not satisfyed? Death stares vs continuously in ye face of every infected Person yt passeth by vs, in every coffin wch is dayly & hourely carried along ye streets: ye Bells never cease to putt vs in minde of our mortality.[24] The custom was in ye beginninge to bury ye Dead in ye night only, now both night and day will hardly be tyme enough to do it,[25] for ye last weeks mortality did too apparently evidence that, that ye Dead was piled in heapes above ground for some houres before either tyme could be gained or place to

---

[23] Defoe may or may not have read Austin and Withers: in either case they serve to authenticate the "Journal."
[24] Cf. the Allin Correspondence, September 2, 1665, "The dolefull and almost universall and continuall ringing and tolling of bells," and Pepys, July 26, "the bell always tolling."
[25] Cf. Pepys, August 12, 1665.

bury them in.''[26] Evelyn gives a not less gloomy picture of the streets when the Plague was at its height. On September 7, 1665, he wrote in his *Diary*: "I went along the city and suburbs from Kent Street to St. James's, a dismal passage, and dangerous to see so many coffins exposed in the streets, now thin of people; the shops shut up, and all in mournful silence, not knowing whose turn might be next." By October 11, conditions were, if possible, even worse, when he recorded that he "went through the whole city, having occasion to alight out of the coach in several places, ... when I was environed with multitudes of poor pestiferous creatures begging alms; the shops universally shut up, a dreadful prospect!"

It is Pepys, perhaps, of all who experienced the year 1665, who wrote down the greatest number and variety of notes concerning the Plague. Some of his experiences rival any of the stories told by Defoe in the *Journal*. There are nearly one hundred entries in the *Diary* relating to the Plague, which, when pieced together, furnish us with a more direct and coherent, as well as more interesting, account of that calamity than does Defoe's narrative. Here, of course, we are concerned only with such records as corroborate Defoe's descriptions of the deserted and sorrowful appearance of the town when the Plague was the hottest. A few excerpts from the *Diary* must suffice. On July 22, 1665, Pepys went from one end of London to the other. This is the impression the journey made upon him: "I to Fox-Hall [Vauxhall], where to the Spring garden; but I do not see one guest there, the town be-

---

[26] Defoe denies this, but is in error.

ing so empty of any body to come thither. Only, while I was there, a poor woman came to scold with the master of the house that a kinswoman, I think, of hers, that was newly dead of the plague, might be buried in the church-yard; for, for her part, she should not be buried in the commons as they said she should. . . . I by coach home, not meeting with but two coaches and two carts from White Hall to my own house, that I could observe; and the streets mightily thin of people.'' Three days later, he went to the 'Change, "which was very thin," and the following week (July 30) he remarked that "it was a sad noise to hear our bell to toll and ring to-day, either for deaths or burials; I think five or six times." On September 14, he summarizes a long list of those of his friends or their families who had but recently died of the Plague, which "do put me into great apprehensions of melancholy." The absence of boats on the Thames was very observable, "and grass grows all up and down White Hall court, and nobody but wretches in the streets!" It is this constant dwelling on the utter desolation and misery in the town that hovers over the reader as he goes through the pages of the *Journal*. So, also, it was the melancholy of it all that so impressed Pepys. On October 16, 1665, he again went to the Exchange, "which is very empty, God knows! and but mean people there. . . . Thence I walked to the Tower; but Lord! how empty the streets are and melancholy, so many sick people in the streets full of sores; and so many sad stories overheard as I walk, every body telling of this dead, and that man sick, and so many in this place, and so many in that."

Again, on October 27, he went through Kent Street, "a miserable, wretched, poor place, people sitting sicke and muffled up with plasters at every 4 or 5 doors." A few days later, however, a new face began to appear on the outlook in London, and Pepys voiced the new joy in, "we end the month merrily," owing to a decrease of over 400 in the weekly Bills. Hopes fluctuated with the weather for several weeks, but the whole tendency from this onward was in the direction of a return to health and healthful activities, and away from dismal scenes and melancholy stories.[27]

Thus far it is apparent that Defoe's materials which he used to illustrate the plain historic facts of the Plague Year were in no sense invented by him for the purpose, but were taken directly from parallel originals, or from stories related to him by the survivors of 1665, as abundantly proved by the duplicate or parallel stories and descriptions, some of which he could have known nothing save from oral accounts. Thus, if we find stories by Pepys (such, for example, the Croom Farm stories), or in the Sancroft, and Patrick Correspondence, similar in all essentials to those in the *Journal*, we are certainly justified in concluding that there was no necessity for Defoe to exercise his genius in inventing stories and conditions representing the facts of the Plague, and that he got all these first-hand from those who, like Pepys, Sancroft and Patrick, experienced them. In other words, Defoe's

[27] Defoe has been criticised (albeit in compliment) to the effect that, for purposes of art, he represented the Plague as ceasing more suddenly and more completely than it did in reality. This is only true as regards the fact, but not Defoe's purpose. Defoe simply followed Hodges.

sources were common and equivalent to these. The proof of this will appear in the next Section wherein the now positively known sources of the *Journal* are quite undistinguishable in all essentials from the foregoing, save in the matter of authentic facts as regards statistics, etc.

II

Where, then, did Defoe find the printed materials for his history of the Plague? In the first place, the statistics of the deaths from the distemper, which are manipulated with much skill by Defoe to awe the reader with the increase, spread, and appalling magnitude of the disease, were taken directly from the Bills of Mortality, first compiled in 1665 as *London's Remembrancer*, by John Bell, one of the Parish Clerks. The same year, John Graunt included these Bills in his *Reflections on the Weekly Bills*. This latter book was reprinted in 1720, and probably furnished Defoe with his figures, as the *Journal* shows indications that its author had read the *Reflections*. It is more than probable, also, that the files of the 1665 "newsbooks" were examined, as I shall show, as these contained the Bills as they appeared each week. As to this important feature of the *Journal* I need only add that, with the exception of two or three slips in copying or in proofreading, Defoe is absolutely faithful to the original Bills. It should be noted that these plainly indicated the progress of the Plague from parish to parish. With a London map before him, together with his accurate acquaintance of the town, Defoe should have had little trouble in evolving his history. But as he did not give himself the time to arrange and organize his materials, the *Journal* is far from being a satisfactory history,—not because of any serious misstatements of fact but rather because of the numerous repetitions and inartistic jumble of the facts.

Next in order should be mentioned the various Orders of the Mayor, the Royal Proclamations, etc., for these, together with the statistics and Hodges's account of the Plague, furnished Defoe with the entire framework of the *Journal,* and much of its tissue. In 1721, J. Roberts, a bookseller, republished a number of 1665 documents which he called *A Collection of very Valuable and Scarce Pieces relating to the last Plague in the Year 1665.* Among other things, this included the "Orders Conceived and Published by the Lord Mayor and Aldermen of the City of London concerning the Infection of the Plague, 1665."[1] These Orders, which Defoe reprinted *verbatim,* occupy ten pages in the *Journal,* or a little over one-thirtieth of the entire book. But their importance is by no means to be measured by the space they occupy; for out of these Orders Defoe evolved a considerable proportion of the remainder of his history. This he accomplished in a manner so skilful as to elude the one who reads the *Journal* for pleasure alone; but when subjected to the scrutiny of the historian it immediately appears what Defoe has done and how he did it. In the first place, he restated, either in a contracted or expanded form, in his own manner, practically every one of these Orders, some of them several times. How confidently could he assume the *rôle* of an Examiner

[1] The same collection contained Dr. Hodges's brief account of the Plague, "in a Letter to a Person of Quality." Defoe made slight use of this in comparison to Hodges's more extended "Account" with which he introduces his "Loimologia."

in 1665, and speak, as one having authority, of the duties of that office, when he had the very printed instructions lying open before him! So, also, all the records respecting the searchers and watchmen, shutting up and marking of houses, burial of the dead, forbidding the use of hackney coaches, keeping the streets clean, killing dogs and cats, regulations concerning public houses, prohibiting plays, duties of Lord Mayor and Aldermen, etc., etc., are but repetitions and variations of these Orders. I say "all the records;" but this is not strictly the whole truth, for Defoe often elaborates and embroiders the facts therein with knowledge gleaned from other fields. Thus, for example, his discussions of the work of the watchmen, the nurses, the doctors, and, above all, the order for shutting up, are all enriched and enlarged from his other sources. On the other hand, he sometimes so closely follows a given Order as to assert positively that it was faithfully executed, as in the case of keeping the streets clean, the prompt burial of the dead, etc., at times a physical impossibility. In these instances, it is very likely that Defoe wished to glorify the name and fame of Sir John Lawrence whose courage and untiring labour, as Lord Mayor during that fateful year, will never be passed over without the highest praise.

By detaching these Orders and scattering them over the pages of the *Journal* in his own style, now expanding them in the manner I have related, now illustrating them with stories coming down from 1665 (inevitable in essence, otherwise the facts would be meaningless),[2] now combining them in quite different relations, Defoe succeeded in padding up a thin volume until it reached the required number of pages to meet trade demands, and, in later times, in deceiving an idle, ignorant, gullible public into the pleasant belief that history is fiction, and that the record of fact, if done by one who can translate himself into his materials and his materials into himself, raises the recorder of those facts from the rank of a clever historian to the exalted position of inventor of the facts.

The *Collection of very Valuable and Scarce Pieces* included also "Necessary Directions for the Prevention and Cure of the Plague in 1665. With divers Remedies of small Charge, by the College of Physicians," which Defoe may have made use of, in respect of the treatment of the disease in its various stages, the care to be taken to prevent the disease from getting to the uninfected, airing goods, fumigating houses, etc. But as all this information could have been had from numerous sources, it would be idle to conjecture which one or ones Defoe actually made use of. That he probably used the "Necessary Directions" is suggested by the fact that he states that they were prepared by order of the Lord Mayor, an inference growing out of the "Orders" just discussed, which did emanate from the Lord Mayor's Office. The "Necessary Directions" came as a result of a Privy Council Order, in response to a Royal mandate.

[2] To illustrate: we have the historic facts about shutting up, dishonest watchmen who could be bribed, people escaping out of shut-up houses, thus scattering the Plague broadcast If these four facts are not mere abstractions, then they appear, as a real story when introduced by the simple device, "I heard of a man," etc.

The other Orders and Proclamations mentioned by Defoe, such as proroguing Parliament, adjourning the Law Courts, removing the Exchequer, forbidding the holding of Fairs, regulating trade, ordering fasts, charities, fires in the streets, etc., were all easily accessible in print. Here also should be included the prohibition by foreign powers of trade with England. I have read all these in 1665 prints, and, of course, Defoe also read them, as neither intuition nor genius could have invented them to correspond to the originals in all respects. And it is here necessary to glance at one of the almost certain sources of the *Journal,*—almost certain, because it contains information which would have been difficult for Defoe to find elsewhere. I refer to the newspaper, or "newsbook," as it was then called. Despite the fact that on the very first page of the *Journal* it is asserted that there were "no such things as newspapers in those days"— a statement so gratuitous as to arouse suspicion—I must believe that Defoe made use of the newspapers of 1665.[3] From the *Newes,* and the *Intelligencer,* both owned and edited by Sir Roger L'Estrange, could be gleaned all the Orders and Proclamations, all foreign and domestic news—the weather, the crops, movements of the fleet, politics, trade, depredations of the Dutch capers, the Bills of Mortality, bounty of the

[3] Professor W. P. Trent, in his article on Defoe ("Cambridge History of English Literature," IX, p. 1), makes the astounding statement that, aside from the "Corantos" (1622-1641) and the Civil War and Commonwealth newsbooks, "there existed no real newspaper, no news periodical, not a pamphlet or newsletter, until the appearance of the 'Oxford Gazette' in 1665." As a matter of fact, the "Gazette" was very much inferior to the "Newes" and the "Intelligencer," which had been published regularly since August 31, 1663. The "Gazette" superseded them in November, 1665.

rich, progress of the Plague throughout the kingdom, superstitious yarns reported from the provinces and abroad (some of which I shall reproduce later), and not least of all, stories of an extraordinary nature concerning the Plague, as, for example, the case of the man who escaped into the country with the Plague upon him, and died within a mile of his destination, and the one who polluted a town by being entertained at a public house—comparable to stories related by Defoe. In the British Museum, in the famous collection of Dr. Burney, there is a complete file of newspapers covering the Plague Year. On the margin of each copy of the *Newes* (after it began to publish the Bills, early in June, 1665), there is a weekly, and total, summary of all burials and of all reported deaths from the Plague. These figures are in ink, and a comparison of them with others known to be Defoe's, shows an identical resemblance in every respect. That these summaries agree with those in the *Journal* proves nothing, for both agree with the Bills. However, one number of the *Newes* has no such summary on the margin. With a sharpened curiosity, we turn to the *Journal* for the corresponding week (ending July 11, 1665), and read that "there died last week 1268 of all distempers, whereof it might be supposed above 900 died of the plague." It is, I believe, the only instance where Defoe guesses at the Bill. But as he might easily have supplied the correct figures by a mere glance at Bell's or Graunt's tables, it would be rash to assert that he actually used the very newspapers in question, however pleasing the idea. On the other hand, it should be remembered that the *Journal* was hastily and carelessly put together from notes which Defoe took no pains to verify. The wonder is that there were not more slips. That he knew of the newspapers of 1665 is almost certain; that he made use of them in writing the *Journal* is highly probable.

For example, the newspapers teemed with the advertisements of quacks. Powders and pills and mixtures, which formerly had done service as sure-cures for all common ailments, immediately became pomanders, electuaries, lozenges, plague waters, sovereign internal balsams, *tabellae chymiatricae, pellulae prophylactica,* etc., etc., all as efficacious for preventing and curing plague as they had been for fevers and whooping-cough. Defoe presents us with four of these, "by way of specimen," and says that he could give you "two or three dozen of the like and yet have abundance left behind," in which statement he was quite within "compass." Not only were the people gulled by high-sounding names, but, as always, they were awed by the authority with which some of these advertisements were vaunted. Thus, in the *Newes* No. 58 (July 27, 1665):

"A sovereign Medicine for the prevention and cure of the *Plague, Fevers,* and *Smal Pox,* invented and practised with rare success by the famous *Doctor John Baptist von Helmont,* is now exposed for sale." Another remedy was named after Lady Kent who had used it in a former plague; one was recommended by Lord Ruthuen; and still another bore the sign-manual of Dr. Thomas Clayton, physician to Charles I. If the quack took on a pompous name and claimed to have practised abroad, his chances of success were greatly enhanced. For example (and this reminds one not only of Defoe's first advertisement, but also of the quack who advertised free advice),

"One Doctor *Stephanus Chrisolitus* a famous Physitian, lately arrived in these parts, having travelled in several Countries which have been affected with the Plague, hath found by experience to be very beneficial (by the blessing of God) for preventing the infection thereof, to eat Raisins of the sun in the morning fasting, and Malaga Raisins either baked or boiled; and this he hath published for the public good."[4]

At the other extreme from this philanthropist was the rascal who advertised a concoction, the chief ingredient of which he audaciously asserted to be pure gold, for which he charged the modest price of twenty shillings the ounce! Other ruses to take in the public were not wanting. As soon as the College of Physicians published the result of their conference as to medicines for the poor, many quacks pounced upon this and traded upon the name, 'as recommended by the College,' etc. However, aside from gulling the public, it probably made little difference in the end, as the College's own preparations proved utterly worthless. Indeed, Kemp (*Brief Treatise* p. 3) classed the College along with the other quacks as publishing "observations which they have met with in the cure of diseases, . . . yet not one medicine found out to preserve the Doctor."[5] Instinctively, we recall

[4] "Newes," No. 42.
[5] In charity, it should be remembered that the doctors at that time had scarcely reached the experimental stage in dealing with plague. Dr. George Thompson, who opened a victim of the Plague, is a rare exception. Dr. William Boghurst also ren-

the names of Burnett, Starkey, Dey, O'Dowd, etc.; and, truly, when we scan the College's "Necessary Directions," we may well appreciate Kemp's sarcastic taunt. Take, for instance, the following (ed. 1721, p. 54) for bringing carbuncles and blains to a head: "Pull off the feathers from the tails of living cocks, hens, pigeons, or chickens, and holding their bills, hold them hard to the botch or swelling, and so keep them at that part until they die; and by this means draw out the poison." Dr. Hodges, himself a thoroughly modern man in his views in many respects, was skeptical as to the efficacy of the powder of the unicorn's horn, but at the same time recommended dried toad's powder! After Kemp's severe criticism we might expect something different from him in the following prescription (*Brief Treatise*, p. 55): "Take crabs' eyes one ounce, burnt hartshorn half an ounce, the black tops of crabs' claws an ounce and a half; make them all into a powder, and take of it one dram in a glass of posset-drink when you go to bed, and drink another draught of posset-drink after, to wash it down."

Not only were the common, ignorant sort taken in by the quacks' specious advertisements, but even the more intelligent also were duped. The case of one Eustace Burneby is in point. Trading upon the name of Dr. Tobias Whitaker, physician in ordinary to Charles II, he secured from Robert Boreman, Rec-

---

dered great service to science by making most careful observations of the distemper in all its stages and under every condition. He visited "40, 50, or 60 patients a day," dressed the sores of 40 a day, ate and drank with the patients, allowed them to breathe in his face, and held them in his arms while they were dying. Cf. "Loimographia," and "Intelligencer" No. 59.

tor of St. Giles's in the Field, and from the sexton,
John Gerey, an affidavit to the effect that in four
houses where divers persons had died of the Plague,
after administering Burneby's powder to the survivors in those houses, not one thereafter died; whereas in houses not using the said powder, "divers have
died, and in many of them the whole family."[6] At
first sight this looks somewhat suspicious, but when we
recall that at that very moment Lord Arlington
(Chief Secretary of State) and the Privy Council
were being completely gulled by the arch-quack himself, one James Angier, who professed to have put a
stop to the infection at Lyons, Paris, Toulouse and other cities, we may readily credit the Rev. Mr. Boreman
with sincerity. Official sanction was given to
Angier's "remedies" and depôts were designated
where they might be had. It was the most stupen-
dous swindle of the whole year.[7]

Likewise the belief in the efficacy of magic phil-
tres, charms, amulets, etc., mentioned by Defoe in this
connection, was not confined solely to the lower classes.
Faith in this superstition still survives and probably
will continue to live as long as man does. Within a
few feet of where I now sit penning these lines, there
is as this moment on the table of an unknown co-
worker no fewer than four or five bogey-frighteners
which are always propped and arranged in precisely
the same relative order and position, before the in-

[6] "Intelligencer," No. 51.

[7] See "Newes," No. 50. Hodges ("Loimologia," p. 22) alludes
to this case, without mentioning names, in most disparaging
terms. It should be observed here that the profession of
physick was at that time divided into two bitterly opposing
camps, one following Galen, the other Hippocrates. To all
outward appearances their practices differed little.

dividual whom they own begins his daily work. They differ much in outward appearance, and, presumably, in satanic virtues; but there they are day after day, day after day, and one imagines that they are similarly placed on a shelf at the foot of the bed, night after night, night after night. And who has not carried a rabbit's foot, pocket-piece, wish-bone, horse-shoe, or the like, for good luck; or worn asafoetida, or some such lovely stuff, to ward off small-pox, or something else? Well, Defoe had any number of examples of 1665 amulets in his own library, or otherwise easily accessible. A few of these may not prove amiss here. Kemp (*op. cit.*, 64) recommends the following: "Take of white and yellow arsenick of each half an ounce, the powder of dried toads two ounces, mercury sublimed, wheat flowre, the roots of dittany, of each three drams, saffron, the fragments of jacynth and emerald, of each one scruple, make them all into powder, and with gum dragon dissolved in rose-water, make them into cakes about the breadth of a shilling, and the thickness of two half crowns, and dry them in the sun, or in an oven after the bread is taken out.

"I need not tell you that you must not eat them, but sew them in a little silk bag, fastening it to a ribbon, and hanging it about your neck, let it be about the middle of your breast." Kemp does not explain just what effect the tablet thus made and worn had, and we must look to other authorities for enlightenment. Fortunately these are numerous. Dr. George Thompson, whom I have mentioned as having dared to dissect a corpse dead of the plague, showed the unmistakeable symptoms of the disease before the operation was finished. He analyzes his own case with much praiseworthy detail, and the treatment thereof. He first had resort to the remedies then commonly used to produce sweating, and then proceeds, "Neither was I wanting to make use of Helmont's xenexton, a toad, the powder of which my dear friend Dr. Starkey gave me, made up in the form of a trochisk of his own ordering: I likewise hung about my neck a large toad dried, prepared not long before in as exquisite a manner as I possibly could, with my own fingers. This toad sewed up in a linnen cloth was placed about the region of my stomach, where after it had remained some hours, became so tumefied, distended (as it were blown up) to that bignesse, that it was an object of wonder to those that beheld it. Had I not felt and seen this swollen dead body of the toad, I should very much have doubted by relation the truth thereof."[8] John Allin is even more explicit as to the working of the toad charm. "Here [in London]," he says, "are many who wear amulets made of the poison of the toad, which, if there be no infection, workes nothing, but upon any infection invading from time to time, raise a blister, wch a plaister heales, and so they are well."[9] The same writer is also responsible for the following rare gem:

"Friend get a piece of angell gold, if you can of Eliz. coine (y^t is ye best), wch is phylosophicall gold, and keepe it allways in yor mouth when you walke out or any sicke persons come to you: you will find strange effect of it for good in freedome of breathing,

[8] "Loimotomia," p. 86.
[9] "Archæologia," xxxvii, p. 6.

&c. as I have done; if you lye wth it in your mouth w^thout yor teeth, as I doe, viz. in one side betweene your cheke and gumms, and so turning it sometimes on one side, sometimes on ye other.''[10]

The superstitions of the people at the time of the 1665 Plague may appear to modern minds as having been exaggerated by Defoe. ''The people,'' he says, ''from what principle I cannot imagine, were more addicted to prophecies and astrological conjunctions, dreams, and old wives' tales than ever they were before or since.'' This is literally true, and, although making excellent use of the fact, early in the *Journal*, to impress upon the reader the apprehensive state of mind in which people found themselves at the outbreak of the Plague, due to the terrifying predictions of astrologers, fortune-tellers, and the like, Defoe barely states the conditions of the time in this respect. That these conditions were, to a certain extent, the result of money-making quacks, as suggested by Defoe, there is no doubt. But the chief explanation is a psychological one: the astrologers (of which no other age produced so many) were quite as much the result of the mental state of the people as the other way about. This view is carried out by the fact that a belief in portents and prodigies was not confined to the ignorant classes alone, but possessed all ranks of society, save the rare few. The almost universal belief at that time—held by the mediæval mind of all times—that the Plague was a special scourge for man's sins (some gave one reason, some another, as suited their political and religious prejudices), was

[10] ''Archælogia,'' xxxvii, p. 15.

but a short step removed from a certain belief in fore-
warnings of that scourge. Upon this predisposition
to ascribe all calamities of whatever nature to super-
natural causes, the astrologers multiplied and bat-
tened.[11] The way in which they fondled and fostered
the superstitious state of mind, already prepossessed
of fantasies, may be seen from the following extract
from Gadbury's *De Cometis* (1665, p. 48):

"Now, although I have a great faith in apparitions of this nature [*i. e.* comets]; and knowing that
melancholy heads, by the strength of fancy and imagination, may conceit they see such things that really
are not: yet, when such fancies shall really possess
the general opinion, it is to be presumed that somewhat more than common is contriving against the gen-
erality of mankind. As we see it in any individual
person that is engaged in any business of concern-
ment, if there be *perturbario mentis,* or (as we used to
say) if his heart misgive him, or that he be in his own
mind perswaded he shall be worsted or come to dam-
age in his undertaking, he is more than half vanquished before he come to the trial. Our fears but
apt and prepare us for the embraces of that mischief
we dread. And indeed the world not of late, vainly
feared such mischiefs as these comets portend; but
as soon as they have begun to fear, they have been
compelled to share therein. I need not instance in the

[11] Appended to "Coelestis Legatus," Gadbury gives a list of forty-
two astrologers "who either are (or were lately) living." This
included the names of "many Reverend Divines, and learned
Physicians." This does not include the "pseudo-Astronomers,
or knap-sack Astrologers, for not only this Age but this great
City swarms with such Cattell." "De Cometis," p. 2. Defoe's
reference to signs bearing the heads of Friar Bacon, Ambrose
Merlin, and Mother (i. e. Ursula) Shipton is self-explanatory:
these names were synonyms of prophecy and magic.

activity of the sword, or the incroaching quality of the
sickness, both which are playing their parts to purpose all Europe over, and will more within a few
years. For the world must know and believe it as a
truth, THAT COMETS ARE NOT GONE AS SOON
AS THEY DISAPPEAR.''

Despite Hodges's assertion (*Loimologia,* p. 4)
that people of the better (*i. e.* more intelligent) sort
gave little credence to such predictions, we read in
Dr. George Thompson's *Loimotomia* (1666, p. 66),
''That comets, or blazing stars do portend some evil
to come upon mortals, is confirmed by long observation and sad experience, as likewise phenomena of a
Parelios, Paraselene, apparitions of *Dracones volantes
& Trahes Scintillae,* new stars, battles fought, and coffins carried through the air, howlings, screechings, and
groans heard about church-yards, also raining of
blood, unwonted matter, &c., all of which having something *extra naturam,* are portentious and prodigious,
all ordained by that good Philanthropos to advertise
us to a timely resipiscence, and prevention of those
evils that hang over our heads.'' And Hodges, notwithstanding his contempt for astrologers, felt compelled (*op. cit.,* p. 31) to acknowledge the certain
''footsteps of an overruling power'' in the Plague of
1665. Even Dr. William Boghurst (*Loimographia,*
1666, *pr.* 1894, p. 20), while branding the prognosti-
cators as ''those curious observers who pretend to bee
most exquisite on the foresight of future contingencies
of good or evile, and a haire shall not wagge without
their observation, and therefore in their yearly pre-
diction fill the world with noyses of warrs, plagues,

destruction, and overthrowes of kingdomes, mon-
archies, that to this [Plague of 1665] said nothing at
all,[12] yet they will name the Starrs to be all in the
fault,"—nevertheless, includes in his signs fore-
shadowing a plague, "Cometts, gleames of Fire, and
fiery impressions in the Aire," "Famine; also warr,"
"ill conditions of the Starrs, if you will believe the
Astrologers," etc.

Of course, the astrologers, without an exception,
looked upon conjunctions, comets, and, indeed, all
exceptional phenomena, as forerunners of evil things,
and comets in particular were terrible presages.
Thus, John Holwell (*Catastrophe Mundi,* p. 40), writing a few years after the Plague and Fire, asserted
that these calamities had been clearly foreshadowed
by the comets of 1664 and 1665 respectively. After
such dire examples, he continues, "what man is he
who dare presume to say that comets are not the pre-
monishers to mankind, of some more than ordinary
Judgment to fall upon them for their sins;" and John
Merrifield (*Castastasis Mundi,* p. 28) is in accord
when he says that comets "proceed not from natural
causes . . . but from Divine Providence, and sent by
Almighty God as tokens of his wrath against mankind
for his sins." But to quote all the 1665 "authorities"
on comets, conjunctions of planets, and other "prodigies," would require volumes. The bookstalls of
that time were literally stuffed with "almanacks," the

---

[12] As a matter of fact, Richard Edlyn did predict both the Plague
of 1665 and the Fire of 1666 ("Prae-Nuncius Sydereus," 72).
It was such lucky (or unlucky) guessing as this that inspired
the ignorant to believe in portents, and thus increased the mis-
chievous apprehensions mentioned by Defoe and the other writers
on the Plague.

result of a popular demand, and it is safe to say that everyone was steeped in their contents. William Lilly (1602-1681), mentioned by Defoe, held the place of preëminence among the astrologers of the day, and, in addition to many prophecies, published his almanacks annually from 1644 until his death. A far greater and more influential man was John Gadbury (1627-1704) who completely combined the careful observations of the scientist with the quack predictions of the astrologer.[18]   As far as his instruments would permit, he exactly measured and recorded the phenomena of the heavens year after year, and then as industriously proceeded to prognosticate their effects. Like his contemporaries, all apparent irregularities of nature were interpreted by him as portents.   Among an infinite variety of choice prodigies seen or heard in the skies, Gadbury enumerates (*Natura Prodigiorum,*

[18] The other names and titles mentioned by Defoe on the same page with Lilly and Gadbury may as well be disposed of here. A book entitled "Come out of her my People" may, or may not, have existed.   As everybody knows, Defoe's quotation is directly from "Revelations," xviii, 4.   He gives his source for "Yet forty days and London shall be destroyed."   The original text ("Jonah," iii, 4) reads, "Yet forty days and Nineveh shall be overthrown."   "Oh the great and dreadful God!" is at once recognised as from "Daniel," ix, 4.   It has been mentioned already that "Woe to Jerusalem" and the flaming sword are from Josephus ("Works," ed. 1773, Bk. vii, ch. 12).   There are any number of "Britain's Remembrancers."   George Withers gave that title to his history of the Plague of 1625.   Again, in 1644, there was published "England's Remembrancer, or a Warning from Heaven," etc.   "Warning" was a common subtitle during that age of prophecies.   Thus, "Prodigies & Apparitions, or England's Warning Pieces," 1643.   This book contains the expression, "fair warning," which may have furnished Defoe with his title.   It also narrated a sufficient number of "prodigies" to supply Defoe with all his materials on that topic.   In one instance, viz., "Poor Robin's Almanack," Defoe never saw more than the title, for this book was a broad burlesque of the astrological trumpery of the times.   For example, Poor Robin records this wisdom for February, 1664: "This month this year hath twenty and nine days in it; now if it had two more it would have thirty and one."   The following month, "the fishmonger's harvest," is filled with a series of puns on plaice, carp, maids, soles, pout, etc.

1660, p. 14) "burials, processions, combats, weapons
of all sorts, crowns and sceptres, flaming swords and
crosses, castles, cities, towers, monsters, comets,
eclipses, etc., etc. He then arranges all these in a
chronological table of "prodigies with their effects,"
extending over forty-six pages and covering the years
from the birth of Christ down to 1660. Blazing stars,
swords and crosses are frequent "causes," followed
by plague, war, famine, etc.

In *London's Deliverance Predicted* (July, 1665),
Gadbury deals directly with the Great Plague in relation to certain "causes." Among these, he specifies
the conjunction of Saturn and Jupiter, October 10,
1663, of Saturn and Mars, November 12, 1664,[14] the
two comets at the close of 1664, and the comet which
appeared early in 1665.[15] Aside from his predictions
in this characteristic book, Gadbury's testimony as to
the outbreak of the Plague in 1664 is of so much interest as to justify its quotation in part. Commenting
on the comets and conjunctions just mentioned, he
says: "By this connexion of causes, it is somewhat apparent that this Pest should have taken its beginning
at the later end of 1664; and truly had not the Winter

---

[14] It will be recalled that Defoe speaks of these two conjunctions
as if they both occurred in 1664. This slip was due to the fact
that he followed Hodges, who did not give dates.

[15] According to the usual account there was but one comet at the
close of 1664. Defoe mentions only one comet in 1664 and one
in 1665, and he deals with these as to appearance, colour, motion,
etc., as presaging symbols of the Plague and Fire respectively.
These descriptions of Defoe's are in direct opposition to those
of M. Adrien Auzout, the eminent French astronomer of the day,
who recorded his observations of one comet in 1664 and one in
1665. Defoe has been accredited with reversing the characteristics of these two comets (cf. E. W. Brayley, ed. "Journal,"
1872, p. 29) "for purposes of heightening the interest." Gadbury, however, ("De Cometis," 31 sq. and "Coelestis Legatus,"
62) has definitely and accurately recorded three comets in all in
1664-5 Two of these exactly fit Defoe's descriptions.

then been so extreamly sharp (it having a frost of almost ten weeks continuance together) to have kept it back, as we knew it did, it had beyond all question broke forth then. Nay, and break forth it did then too, as my self can experimentally testify, having been personally visited with it at Christmas that year. And my good friend Mr. Josias Westwood the chirurgeon (whose assistance I then craved, and advice I followed (I bless God) to my preservation) hath told me since that many of his patients at that time were afflicted with the same distemper, and yet obtained cure against it, the air being then so friendly to nature, and an enemy unto the Pestilence. And besides, it was but president in people to keep it from the knowledge of the world (since few or none dyed thereof) as long as they could; for we find that it came to a discovery soon enough to amaze and terrifie the whole Nation, and hath bid fair for the ruin of trade of all kinds in this great and populous city.''

That the astrologers, with their nativity diagrams, ''airy triplicities,'' etc., had succeeded thoroughly in bamboozling the people is evidenced by various newsletters from every portion of England and the Continent, on the appearance of the first comet in December, 1664. Many of these letters, after relating the facts respecting the comet, turn to the ''wisemen'' and ''artists'' ''to enquire what it may portend.'' A letter from York (dated December 18, 1664) to Gadbury closes with the request that, ''you will not only oblige me, but many of my friends hereabouts, very much, if you will but vouchsafe your opinion in a line or two from your own hand, what this strange new Star may portend.''[16]   Some of these letters concerning the comet reported other occompanying "prodigies," comparable to some of those mentioned by Defoe. In a newsletter from Hamburgh, December 24, 1664 (published in *Newes*, January 5, 1665), we read that ''The great Comet lately seen here, appears no longer with us; but here is now another, much less then the formar, rising South-East, and setting North-West. They write from Vienna by the last [mail], of a great Comet seen there also, shewing itself first from the East, and pointing toward Hungary. There has been likewise seen in the ayre the appearance of a Coffin, which causes great anxiety of thought among the people.'' From Erfurt came still more alarming accounts. "We have had our part here," so runs the letter, "of the Comet, as well as other Places, besides which, here have been other terrible Apparitions and Noises in the ayre, as Fires, and sounds of Canon, and Musket-shot; and here has likewise appear'd several times the resemblance of a Black man, which has made our Sentinels to quit their Posts; and one of them was lately thrown down by him from the top of the Wall.''

As intimated elsewhere in the course of this essay, it is likely that Defoe may have got at least some of his superstitious stories, as for instance the coffin apparition, from the newspapers; but as all these "prodigies" were common to the superstittion of the times,

[16] The strong belief in, and the fearful apprehensions occasioned by, predictions of calamities, is well illustrated by the prophecy of a mere child, when the Plague was at its height in 1665, that the mortality would increase "till 18,317 dye in a weeke (which all endeavors are used to conceale)." "Archæologia" xxxvii, 15. In Seville, an astrologer was "clapt up" because some of his predictions of dire events came true, and the authorities wished to allay the apprehensions of the people.

it cannot always be said with certainty that any given original was Defoe's source of authority. For example, Gadbury copied the Hamburgh letter just quoted (*De Cometis,* p. 48) and as it is comparatively certain that Defoe had read Gadbury he may have found it there. In the case of the flaming sword in the *Journal,* as Defoe had quoted the Josephus book a few pages earlier, we may assume that authority to be the source of that superstition. At any rate, even the few extracts and references which I have given to the superstitions of the times, and the influence of the astrologers in perturbing the public mind with apprehensions of dreadful and dreaded events, will serve to indicate what a storehouse of materials Defoe had to draw from in writing this part of his *Journal.* Defoe possessed, among other books of a similar character, the "Prophecies" of Notradamus which had been republished in English by Lilly in 1651, and again by Holwell in 1682. Both these editions contained the numerous drawings or "hieroglyphics" of the original. Moreover, besides the chronicles (of which Defoe owned three or four) and the numerous almanacks, already mentioned, there were the easily accessible works of Wing, Wharton, Tacke, Mother Shipton, Ashmole, Ardee, Saunders, Booker, Marsh, Wells, Flood, Hopton, Vaux, etc., *ad infinitum.*

For the fortune-telling quacks, the astrologer quacks had as much contempt as Defoe had for both. Gadbury says of them (*op. cit.* 164) that "so common and general are these catching errors become, that it is now a most difficult and hard matter to distinguish a plow-man from a natural philosopher from his dis-

course. And . . . as in former times it was a rare matter to find seven wise men in the world, it is now as difficult and troublesome to discover the same number
of fools. Every man, almost, that hath scarcely arrived at the happiness of reading a Horn-book, accounts all things that come within the parcimeter or
compass of discourse beneath him and his genius . . .
that treateth not of the raising of spirits of some
periapt, amulet, or magical charm or spell." Of these
fortune-tellers there were two classes,—those who
for "fame and money impose upon the understanding
of simple-minded, credulous people," and, secondly,
"a company of poor, melancholy, crack-brain'd shal-
low-soul'd creatures, born as well to spread lies and
impostures as to credit and believe them." (This
from the author of *Natura Prodigiorum!*) In which
of these classes Gadbury would catalogue the following, I will leave to the reader to decide. He relates
(*op. cit.* 174) that Sir K. Digbie once trapped "that
Arch-pretender, Dr. Lamb" in his knavery, and
threatened to kick him down the stairs; upon which
circumstance he comments: "I am of belief the application of this story will reach (if not over-reach) the
consciences and practices of some among us that wear
the golden name of Astrologers who very commonly,
under pretence thereof, make use of a Christal, and
other pretended cheats and shifts, to gull the sillier
sort of people. Nay, they are made use of sometimes
to persons at very great rates (viz. six pounds a call,
as they knavishly call it) even to their undoing, and to
the great scandal of Astrologie (which, as it is dealt
with, is the only over-cheat of these times) and, in-

deed, to the shipwreck and ruin of the practitioner's conscience, honesty, and good name. Nay, the villainy is grown so rife and common now among us, that he is not worthy (almost) to be deemed an astrologer, that cannot stretch both his conscience and skill, like unto those persons touched, who by their practices should be of Cacus's progeny, because they so eminently pretend to make with him,

Candida de nigris, & de candentibus arra.''

So much for that feature of the *Journal* dealing with the superstition and gullibility of the people. Of a different character from statistics, proclamations, advertisements, almanacks, etc., are the sources treating of the history of the Plague,—its origin, its first appearance in London, its progress, ravages and decline—which supplied Defoe with that necessary element of his narrative. Too much importance cannot be attached to these sources, as they brought to Defoe something more than mere facts, they lent him language and "atmosphere." In 1722, there were no fewer than two score volumes on the subject of plague, some mere pamphlets, some treating only of the prevention and cure of the disease, while others combined the treatment with the history of plague. About one-half of these volumes refer to the Plague of 1665, while some of them ante-date it. It is needless to go over the list of these, as the mass of them were of little use to Defoe in the composition of the *Journal*. Kemp's *Brief Treatise,* the author of *Golgotha,* the author of *Shutting up Infected Houses,* and a few others mentioned in Section I contributed certain aspects: but, in the main, Defoe relied upon very few sources for the skeleton of his narrative. Foremost amongst these stands Dr. Nathaniel Hodges, so frequently mentioned in the course of this discussion. That his work was freely drawn upon by Defoe has long been known to scholars, but, inasmuch as no one hitherto has had the curiosity, or courage, to analyze the *Journal* with reference to *Loimologia,* the tremendous debt which the former owes to the latter has never been fully appreciated. Hodges's "Historical Account" fills less than thirty octavo pages; yet Defoe not only took over practically every item contained in Hodges's account, but in almost every instance followed him so closely as to copy his errors, and repeated his subject matter so many times that the materials borrowed from *Loimologia* gave Defoe his starting point no fewer than one hundred and twenty-five times,—and this does not take into account the numerous instances where the narration or discussion (as *e. g.* of shutting up) extends over a number of pages, such cases being counted only once in the sum total! This statement appears incredible, but any one who will take the pains to analyze ,Hodges's "Account," and then the *Journal,* will find it true "within compass,"—albeit some idols may get broken in the process.

Before me as I write I have such an analysis, with the result as stated. Even the digressionary style of Hodges is followed by Defoe, and the former's account of the origin of the 1665 Plague might easily be mistaken for the opening paragraph of the *Journal,* both as to style and content.[17] A synopsis of Hodges's ac-

[17] I have traced the progress of the distemper over Europe before it got to England, but space forbids going into this. Suffice it to say that Defoe's account is strictly historical.

count of the Plague will serve to illustrate the extent of Defoe's reliance upon that single source, a brief outline of which follows. According to Hodges, the distemper came to Holland in a parcel of infected goods from Smyrna, and from Holland to England where it suddenly appeared in London near the close of 1664, when three died of it. Some people took alarm and moved into the City; wild rumours and predictions terrified the common sort whose very fears precipitated the distemper. Their apprehensions were further augmented by the appearance of the comet and the conjunctions of Saturn and Jupiter, and Saturn and Mars, followed by the terrifying predictions of astrologers. Hodges deplores this fearmongering. A hard frost, lasting three months, lulled people into a belief of security; but about Christmas Hodges is called to a case which he pronounced to be plague. With the breaking up of the frost in the Spring of 1665, the disease reappeared and soon gained ground. The Magistrates issued a shutting-up order, but the efficacy of the practice is questioned, and, on the whole, condemned, though there is something to be said on the other side, especially at the first appearance of the distemper. It was decreed that all infected houses must be marked with a red cross and the "Lord have mercy" sign over the door, a guard placed outside to prevent the inmates from escaping, and to pass in food and medicine to those shut up. The establishment of a forty-days quarantine (according to the printed "Orders," it was only four weeks), to be counted from the last one infected in a shut up house, caused consternation and mischief, for this order and the "tragical mark over the door" frightened many neighbours away who might have been of service in saving lives. The dishonest and murderous practices of wicked nurses cannot be too strongly condemned. A strange symptom of the disease was an insane or perverse pleasure the infected manifested of breathing into the faces of the well.[18]

The Plague "doubtfully reigned" throughout May and June, "sometimes raging in one part, and then in another." The minds of the people fluctuated with the Bills: "as often as the funerals decreased, great hopes were conceived of its [the Plague's] disappearance, then on a sudden again their increase threw all into dejection." This caused the inhabitants to leave precipitously, and they "flocked in such crowds out of town, as if London had quite gone out of itself." In an effort to stem the tide of devastation, the authorities ordered monthly fasts and public prayers, and commanded the College of Physicians to prepare some remedy in English for the poor people, who were the chief sufferers in this calamity. But their labours proved in vain. A number of eminent physicians tendered their assistance; yet, although the weather conditions were good and food plentiful,[19] the ravages of the disease continued unabated. In July and August it changed its former slow and languid pace to a swift and terrible

18 Mead ("Short Discourse," 8th ed., p. xvii) repeats this statement and offers an explanation for the cause of the symptom. Defoe rehashes the same explanation, but, in a sort of mock piety, does not see how the fact can be "reconciled to religion."
19 Hodges is here misleading. He himself calls it the "poor's Plague," and all the sources (and Defoe) agree that the poor suffered greatly for the very necessities of life. The constant and pathetic appeals for charity support the fact: if food was plentiful it was not free.

slaughter, so that 3,000, 4,000, or 5,000 died in a week,—once 8,000. The calamity was inexpressible: carcasses lay unburied, one heard dying groans and ravings of delirium, relations and friends bewailing their losses, and, at the same time, anticipating their own sudden end; death was the sure midwife to all children; the newly-wed died in their first embrace; some ran about staggering like drunk and fell dead in the street; others lay comatose, half-dead, still others fell dead in the market while purchasing the necessities of life; and who "would not burst with grief to see the stock of a future generation hang upon the breasts of a dead mother?"[20]

The Plague spared no order, age, or sex. The divine perished in the exercise of his priestly duties, the physician died administering his own antidotes. Of the female sex most died,[21] and few children escaped. Inheritances passed to three or four heirs in as many days; there were not enough sextons to bury the dead; the bells were hoarse with continual tolling; the burial places were inadequate, and so large pits were dug in waste grounds and thirty or forty bodies were thrown in at one time. Those who attended funerals of friends one evening were often buried the next.

The Court being at Oxford, the City authorities ordered fires built in the streets for three days together. The advice of the physicians was against this,

[20] Defoe worked over this statement into the story (about the middle of the "Journal") beginning, "I could tell here dismal stories of living infants being found sucking the breasts of their [dead] mothers," etc.
[21] Nearly all the authorities make this statement, but the Bills of Mortality show only a slight excess of women over men.

and the sequel proved them right, for more than 4,000 died in one night following the fires.[22] The practices of chemists and quacks also aggravated the ravages of the disease. "They thrust into every hand some trash or other under the disguise of a pompous title." Hardly any escaped who trusted their remedies, but as a partial vengeance for their wicked impostures, "they were caught in the common ruin."[23] Experiments with foreign medicines also proved disasterous.

The contagion spread to the country, especially to the towns along the Thames, owing to infected goods being carried up it.

The height passed, "the Plague by leisurely degrees declined," and, besides, it was now less fatal, for a greater proportion of the infected recovered than in midsummer. People grew less fearful, one of another, and after a time "a dawn of health appeared as sudden and as unexpected as the cessation of the following conflagration."[24] This was due to the less malig-

[22] Defoe doubts the accuracy of this, and it is not corroborated by any other source. That at least 10,000 a week died at one stage in the Plague is not questioned by the author of the "Journal."

[23] Defoe paraphrases Hodges thus: "Some fancied they were all swept away in the infection to a man, and were for calling it a particular work of God's vengeance." It will be remembered also that Defoe points out that a number of eminent physicians were carried away by the Plague. Hodges (p. 15) says eight or nine physician died (some of these I have already mentioned). Defoe had a list of five physicians and eighteen surgeons. Pepys (October 16, 1665) heard that in Westminster they were all dead save one apothecary. John Allin on September 14, 1665, wrote that seven score doctors, apothecaries and surgeons "are all 'dead of this distemper in and about ye city." ("Archæologia," xxxvii, p. 10). While Dr. George Thompson was suffering from plague (after dissecting a corpse), his two colleagues, Drs. Dey and Starkey, died. Of this Thompson wrote, "At that very time [August, 1665] . . . two of my most esteemed consorts, Dr. Joseph Dey and Dr. George Starkey, two pillars of chimical physick, were both reposed in their graves before I knew of their deaths." ("Loimotomia," 96). Starkey ascribed his death to the taking an over-draught of beer.

[24] It is this statement, which Defoe merely takes over from Hodges, that has been apologized for as "for purposes of art."

nant nature of the distemper. And, just as at the beginning, all other diseases seemed to go into the Plague, so now, the Plague degenerated into other contagious diseases. In December, people crowded back to town as eagerly as they formerly ran away, and that too without fear, lying in beds but recently occupied by the infected. Shops were again opened, and business took on a normal tone. Cheerfulness and courage became more manifest, and, before long, the ravages of the Plague were scarcely discernible. Some compute that over 100,000 died of the distemper. It broke out again in the Spring of 1666, but was readily conquered.

Aside from the few disagreements (indicated in the footnotes) the foregoing summary of Hodges's "Historical Account of the Plague" might readily be mistaken for a condensed outline of Defoe's history; and, truly, such it is so far as it goes. If we but add to this the statistical and other documentary data, and the illustrative stories and descriptions of the town and people during the Plague, we should then have the *Journal* complete. It is here, of course, that the stickler for the fictional element in the *Journal* comes in with his theory; and it must be confessed that the most effective feature of Defoe's history is the use he makes of the illustrative stories and dismal scenes to arouse in the reader a feeling of the apalling calamity, and an overwhelming pity for the sufferers. But here again there was absolutely nothing original with Defoe. Not for one moment can his work be compared, in richness of materials, sincerity, and eloquent pathos, with one of his chief sources, namely, Thomas

Vincent's *God's Terrible Voice in the City*, which I have had occasion to mention more than once. Vincent was one of those Non-conforming preachers who had been ousted from their livings by the Act of August 24, 1662, and, by the Act of March 24, 1665, banished five miles from all Corporations. He was one of several such ministers mentioned by Defoe who remained in London during the Plague and filled the empty pulpits made vacant by Conformists running away from their flocks.[25] Naturally, Vincent saw the Plague in the light of a just vengeance sent from God on his political and religious enemies,—especially on those ministers who had run away, and Defoe may well have had him in mind, among others, whose "sermons rather sank than lifted up the hearts of their hearers."[26] So, too, Vincent's outcries against blasphemy may have suggested to Defoe the sermon on the same text. However, all this was common to the ser-

[25] Among those Presbyterians who took up their ministerial duties again during the Plague were, Vincent, Allin, Chester, Franklin, Grimes, Turner, and Janaway (who died of plague). That there was a very strong feeling against the regular clergy for running away is evident on every hand. The Sancroft Correspondence illustrates this. On February 4, 1666, Pepys wrote in his "Diary," "The Lord's day; and my wife and I the first time together to church since the plague, and now only because of Mr. Mills his coming home to preach his first sermon; expecting a great excuse for his leaving the parish before anybody went, and now staying till all are come home, but he made a very poor and short excuse, and a bad sermon." It would be a great mistake and gross injustice, however, to suppose that all the regular clergy left their charges. 'Tis true, most did, including Bishop Henchman and Dean Sancroft; but some of the rectors, vicars, and canons stuck to their posts, such as Patrick, Clifford, Bing, Masters, Simpson, Morris, Portington, Griffith (who died of plague), Overing, Horton, Merriton, and others.

[26] Defoe had a splendid choice from which to reach this conclusion. Take for example, this reviving excerpt from Vincent's funeral sermon on Abraham Janaway, Sept. 18, 1665: "Look! do you not see the mouth of the pit open, and before it be shut again, you may be put in; you see the righteous perish, but you are in danger of a far worse perishing; . . . their souls are taken away by angels, and conveyed to heaven, but when your bodies drop into the grave, your soul will be dragged by

mons of the time, as well as to Defoe's own time, and special sources for pious exhortations need not be sought. Solomon Eagle, as already pointed out, had his prototype in John Gibson, the 17th Century Quaker fanatic; but Vincent might just as well have furnished Defoe with the substance of Solomon's execrations. Likewise, the penitent sinners, so frequently mentioned in the *Journal*, came directly from *God's Terrible Voice*. Indeed, an analysis of this book, as in the case of *Loimologia*, reveals the fact that Defoe made use of it for all it would produce: in no fewer than sixty instances in the *Journal* may we trace the origins to Vincent, and, as in the case of the materials borrowed from Hodges, there are many repetitions. As much of the materials of the *Journal* are common to *God's Terrible Voice* and *Loimologia*, mention here need only be made of the particulars with which Vincent, and only Vincent, supplied Defoe. The arousal of sinners to repentance has just been referred to. It is more particularly the aspect of the people and the desolation caused by the pest, so graphically portrayed by Vincent, that furnished Defoe with one of his chief assets. In *God's Terrible Voice* he found all that was necessary to express the apprehensions and fears, the altered, scared looks of the poor people, especially after the rich had deserted the town and the order for shutting up and marking the infected houses had been issued; shops shut up, grass growing in the streets, few people

devils into hell,'' etc. Oddly enough, however, this seems to have been the sort of thing the poor frightened creatures of that time hungered for and crowded to the churches to hear, regardless of the danger of the infection.

abroad; "not one house in an hundred but is infected,"—a fearful slaughter, whole families dead, the church-yards stuffed full; cries and groans of the sick and dying, the afflicted in their frenzy rising out of bed roar at the window or run forth naked into the streets,—one man burnt himself to death in bed. Defoe made use of all this over and over again, never failing to impress the awfulness of the times by means of pious ejaculations, borrowed along with the materials from the sources. One of the many details in the *Journal* taken straight over from Vincent is the story of the wag who advertised a "pulpit to be let," after the minister had run away. Also, Defoe like Vincent, moralizes on that perennial quality in human nature, that during the calamity all differences of opinion were silenced—in the presence of the common enemy—but after the gravest dangers were passed, the old religious quarrels broke out again and people resumed the habit of their old sins. As in the case of Hodges, Defoe let nothing he could use from Vincent escape his net.

The remention of Defoe's religious piety makes it necessary to dispel another myth respecting the *Journal,* or rather respecting Defoe. It will be recalled at once that Defoe, that is, Defoe's sadler who relates the story, was much disturbed as to whether he should remain in town, look after his business, and trust in God, or, like others who were able, flee to the country.[27] Like many another distracted person of

[27] It will be recalled that the sadler's brother argued with him as to the folly of remaining and pointed as example to the predestinarian view held by the Turks to their undoing. The reference to the Turk in this connection was very common. Cf. Kemp, "Brief Treatise," p. 15, a copy of which Defoe owned.

that day, he wavered now this way, now that, not knowing what to do. Finally, one evening after much worry about the question, he, as if by accident, or divine guidance, opened the Bible at the 91st Psalm. This settled all his doubts,—he would remain! One editor of the *Journal,* in an excess of devotion to Defoe's fertile genius, gives vent to his feelings in, "Nothing could be more natural than the account of the sadler's uncertainty whether he should leave London, . . . and when he opened his Bible he lighted on the words," etc. "From that moment he resolved to stay, knowing that whatever happened he was in God's hands." Well, now, it was rather necessary that Defoe should devise some means to keep his sadler in town—otherwise the narrative would have ended somewhat abruptly. Of course, any schoolboy could have had him remain without inventing any arguments about the business; but such a simple process would have branded the author as a novice, to say the least. Now, the "lighting on the words" gives distinction and an air of naturalness to the narrative. As a matter of fact, nearly all the writers on the subject from the time of David onwards have gone over the arguments about fleeing the plague. One has but to open any book on the pest to learn this,—Bezè, Gadbury, Kemp, Patrick, Austin, author of *Golgotha,* etc., etc. As for the Psalms, they have always been resorted to for consolation in times of trouble in general, and in cases of the plague in particular. One author makes twenty-six biblical references in one connection, the list being headed by the 91st Psalm which reappears three times *(Golgotha,* p. 14). C. Conraden wrote a poem devoted entirely to that Psalm (1633), and Theodore Bezè, in a *Shorte learned and pithie Treatise* (1580) treats of it *in extenso* in respect of fleeing from the pestilence. To come nearer home, we may dismiss the whole matter at once by referring to Symon Patrick's *Consolatory Discourse* (1665, p. 30) wherein he not only cites the 91st Psalm, but quotes that portion, and only that portion, repeated by Defoe. It would have been nothing wonderful if Defoe, with his knowledge of the Bible, had *turned* to the passage in question, but to credit him with *lighting upon* it is sheer nonsense. As we have caught him so many times red-handed in the act of appropriating materials for the *Journal*, it is safe to suggest that he took the quotation directly from Patrick, with whose writings he was well acquainted. This example is fairly illustrative of the *Journal* as a whole, so far as it relates to Defoe's originality in creating the narrative of the Plague.

III

That some slips and errors should have crept into a history of the nature of the *Journal* was inevitable. But these are comparatively few, generally of slight importance, and due, in nearly every instance, to haste or to misleading sources. I have already taken account of some of these, and they need only be mentioned here in way of summary. That there were printed newspapers in those days, Defoe must have been aware. Likewise, it would seem that he should have known that microscopes had been in use for a generation before the Plague Year. On the other hand, I have found no indication that they were brought into use in connection with the treatment of the distemper of 1665. It was, however, sheer carelessness or haste that accounts for wrong dates and inaccurate statistics. For example, almost on the first page of the *Journal* Defoe mentions two Frenchmen who died of the Plague in Long Acre, or thereabouts, in December, 1664, and shortly afterwards says there was only one, a statement which he repeats. On the second page it appears that none died of the disease from December, 1664 until "about the 12th of February" following; near the end of the *Journal* the 9th of February is given. The same kind of carelessness if found respecting the number of pesthouses: in three places Defoe says there was only one, in another place he says two. The latter statement is correct. The number that died of the Plague at the Westminster pesthouse is given as 159, which should read 156; but this is evidently the proofreader's error.[28] One table in the *Journal* is misleading, namely, the one showing the number of deaths from August 22 to September 26, 1665, which was 38,195. The impression left is that this represents the deaths from the Plague, whereas it represents the total number of deaths. Defoe should have added, "whereof 31,331 of the Plague." In one instance, his figures are entirely at variance with the Bills: in demonstrating the fact that many who died of the distemper were set down to other diseases, he records for 1664, "child-bed, 189; abortive and still-born, 458." This should read, "child-bed, 250; abortive and still-born, 503." For the week ending July 4, 1665, Defoe says that "not one person died of plague in all Stepney parish." The Bills returned two that week for Stepney. The following week he estimated the number from plague at 900; the Clerks reported 725. This is Defoe's only venture at an estimate of the number of deaths from the pestilence in a given week; his other figures are taken directly from the Bills.

It has already been shown that the error in the *Journal* respecting the dates of the planet conjunctions was due to the fact that Defoe's authority (Hodges) did not indicate the years in which they occurred, and Defoe assumed that they both immediately preceded the outbreak of the Plague. As to the movements of the Court, he was entirely at sea,—another slip due to Hodges's indefiniteness. Defoe says

[28] In checking up errors in the "Journal" I have used the 1st edition.

that the Court removed to Oxford in June, and returned to town soon after Christmas. The newsbooks of the day furnish us with the exact movements of the Court. On July 2, 1665, Charles II and his suite went to Hampton Court (the Queen Mother went to France a few days earlier). They remained at Hampton Court until July 28. As a greater means of precaution, on that date the King moved towards Salisbury, first visiting Portsmouth and Isle-of-Wight, arriving at Salisbury on August 1. On September 15, Charles began a Royal Progress, in which was included, in order, Poole, Lulworth, Weymouth, Portland, and Dorchester. The King returned to Salisbury on September 21. The pest appearing there about this time, the Court hastily removed to Oxford on the 25th of the month. There Parliament was convened on October 9, and there the Court remained until January 27, 1666, when it came back to Hampton Court. Five days later (February 1) Charles and his followers returned to Whitehall, having been away exactly seven months.

As I have already mentioned, the order to the College of Physicians was a royal command, and did not come from the Mayor as stated by Defoe. As to the good work of the Mayor and Aldermen, Defoe seems to have been obsessed with the idea that they must have scrupulously enforced all orders emanating from them, such as keeping the street clean, burying the dead, etc. As a matter of fact they accomplished almost superhuman results, under the circumstances and conditions of the times, but nothing so complete as Defoe asserts. In this connection he mentions charities (inasmuch as the Lord Mayor was largely responsible for their distribution) and states that £17,800 were distributed to Cripplegate in one week. This is the only instance of gross exaggeration I have found in the *Journal*. While the whole truth can never be known as to the amounts distributed to the poor during the Plague, as a great deal of money was sent to private individuals, rectors, curates, etc., of which no public account was kept, it is extremely doubtful whether all of the parishes of London taken together ever received as much as £17,800 in one week in charities. Defoe also asserts that the King ordered £1,000 distributed weekly, but I know not his authority. The City of London, however, did vote £600, and many of the parishes increased the rates heavily to meet the emergency. Even so, the contributions from all quarters fell far short of meeting the necessitous conditions, and after the distemper spread to the one hundred and thirty parishes of the City and suburbs it was precious little that any one parish received at one time.

A few more scattering details will suffice to cover the remaining slips in the *Journal*. Defoe was not aware that the plague got into the fleet, simply because every effort was made to conceal the fact; hence his error in stating the contrary.[29] So, also, as to the army, he says, "as to soldiers, there were none to be found," etc. In a manner this was true, when we consider that the London of 1665 was not the London of 1914-1919. They were quartered in Hyde Park in

[29] For proof that the distemper got aboard the ships, see "Cal. State Papers" Dom., December 25, 1665 and February 2, 1666.

tents, and returned to town on November 6, 1665.[30]
Again, Defoe erroneously states that the Exchange
was kept open during the Plague. It was closed for
repairs during August and September, 1665.[31] As
for the impression we get from the *Journal* that all the
astrologers were carried away by plague, a number
of the leading ones, as Lilly and Gadbury, lived for a
number of years after 1665 and continued their predictions to the last. In a like manner, Defoe misleads
us when he states that "some of the ministers did visit
the sick at first and for a little while, but it was not to
be done;" from which we infer that after the infection reached its height, they had to abandon their
work. Patrick, Allin, Bing, Vincent, Tillison, and
many others, stuck to their posts throughout, as I have
already shown. A similar wrong impression is left as
regards the fires that were built in the streets, in com-
pliance with the Lord Mayor's order of September 2,
1665. Defoe mentions only fifteen places where fires
were built: the order provided for one fire to every
twelve houses (*i. e.* six houses on either side of the
street).[32] All discrepancies respecting the weather,
winds, drought, progress of the distemper, etc., arise
out of corresponding confusions in Defoe's sources;
statements of this character were based by him on authority, and, besides, the element of error in these respects is so slight as to be virtually negligible.[33]

[30] See letter from Symon Patrick to Elizabeth Gauden, dated November 7, 1665. "Add. MSS." 5810.
[31] "Newes," Nos. 60 and 76.
[32] Cf. "Intelligencer" No. 72.
[33] As illustrations of similar discrepancies, see Thompson, "Loimotomia," 1666, p. 67; Boghurst, "Loimographia," 1666, p. 29;
Withers, "A Precaution relating to the Present Time," 1665,
p. 66.

Of much greater importance than the trivial errors recorded above, is the question of style and method employed by Defoe in the *Journal;* for these have borne a considerable part in getting the name of fiction attached to the book. In the first place, of course, stands the very apparent fact that the narrative is in the first person. To descant upon the charm, the sense of reality, the "atmosphere," which this lends to the book would not only be trite, but altogether superfluous. Little artful tricks of style as, "I saw both these stars," "business led me out sometimes to the other end of the town," "I will not be positive whether he said forty days or a few days," "I met this creature several times in the streets," etc., etc., grip the reader immediately, according to a psychological process appreciated by every one. Had the history of the Plague been written in the usual style of the dry-as-dust historian, the number of readers would have been comparatively small.[84] This style had already been mastered by Defoe, hence, it was applied to the *Journal* for reasons of convenience and taste as well as business. All that concerns us here is that the employment of the first person in the narrative in no sense interferes with the authenticity of the facts recorded. I have already made mention of the story of the carpenter, sailor, and soldier, and have shown that, inasmuch as the integral parts of that story are true, the exception is only apparent, not real. The same is true of the stories growing out of documents, such as

[84] The continuator of Dr. Gideon Harvey's account of the Plague (as "City Remembrancer," 1769) compiled the work from sources and authorities (including the "Journal"), and, hence, is equally reliable as Defoe,—yet who reads Harvey's account?

the Orders, Proclamations, etc.,—either the stories are authentic (I have quoted parallels) or else the documents are without meaning. Any one writing a history of the Plague of 1665 in the third person directly from the original sources would produce a result equivalent to, and in all essentials identical with, Defoe's *Journal.* That a history be written in the first person is not sufficient grounds for classing it with fiction: so far as authenticity is concerned, the style is of no importance whatever. Moreover, I have more than once pointed out that many of the best effects in the *Journal* are not due to the first person, nor are they of Defoe's making, but are paraphrases or direct copies of the original sources.

The most curious thing about the use of the first person in narrating the events of the Plague Year is not that such a style makes the book more interesting to read, but that it served to cover up the most egregious faults known to literature,—digressions, incoherencies, involved and cumbrous expressions, tiresome repetitions,—all of which made it possible for the author to compile a mass large enough to be called a book. A striking example of this is the "as-I-said-before" habit, responsible for scores of needless repetitions in the *Journal,* as many as three or four—sometimes more—of these appearing in the same paragraph, and all referring to the same thing. Innumerable samples of this mannerism may be sighted by casually turning over the leaves of the *Journal.* The repetitions of discussions and comments regarding the progress of the Plague, treatment of the patients (shutting up, watchmen, nurses, etc.), work of the

officers, etc., are less obvious, because they are scattered about in paraphrase and altered expressions.
So hard put to it was Defoe to make a marketable book
that he is forced to repeat his stories. Thus Solomon
Eagle is made to do service three times, as follows:
(a) "I suppose the world has heard of the famous
Solomon Eagle, an enthusiast. He, though not infected at all but in his head, went about denouncing
of judgment upon the city in a frightful manner,
sometimes quite naked, and with a pan of burning
charcoal on his head." (b) "The famous Solomon
Eagle . . . had predicted the plague as a judgment,
and ran naked through the streets, telling the people
it was come upon them to punish them for their sins."
(c) "The famous Solomon Eagle, the naked Quaker I
have mentioned, prophesied evil tidings every day,"
etc. The repetitions of expressions calculated to make
the conditions of the times more realistic are too
numerous to mention. "Dismal scenes," with its
many variations, has been mentioned. The folly of
people rushing back to town as precipitously as they
ran away is condemned a half-dozen times in almost
precisely the same language. He speaks of this fool-
hardiness as "precipitous courage," "unwary conduct," "imprudent, rash conduct," "rash and fool-
ish conduct," "audacious boldness," etc., in each case
repeating the consequences.

How the pest originated in Long Acre and spread
from thence is retold four times in the *Journal*. Even
after he has almost concluded—or rather after the
book should long have been concluded—Defoe starts
over again "how it began at one end of the town."

The discussion of shutting up, with the good and bad effects attending the practice, occurs no less than ten distinct times, some of these involving as many as fifteen or eighteen pages, not to mention the innumerable repetitions within these repetitions. An account of the distractions of victims roaring at the window, running about naked, etc., appears sixteen times; the alleged misrepresentations of the Bills of Mortality thirteen times; the good work of the Magistrates twenty-one times. The same kind of analysis could be applied, with varying results, to the other features of the *Journal*. These tiresome repetitions comprise two-thirds or more of the volume, and, after taking into account every addition of fact or feeling to be found in them, they might be reduced to one-fourth or one-fifth of the space they now occupy without rendering the value of the history less by one iota. The only purpose they serve—in addition to swelling the book's size—is to impress on the imagination the horrors of the Plague. Even so, the emphasis is so much overdone that it loses its force. Viewed from the point of style and art, the work is execrable. To make it perfectly clear that I have not exaggerated in this matter of repetitions in the *Journal*, I will here reproduce a number of them in relation to the unconscious spreading of the disease by people going about with the infection upon them but they not aware of it. Other examples, as above, would show similar results.

(a) "[Often, people escaping from shut-up houses], having an uninterrupted liberty to go about, but being obliged still to conceal their circumstances, or perhaps not knowing it themselves, gave the distemper to others, and spread the infection in a dreadful manner, as I shall explain further hereafter." p. 84.[85]

(b) "Now it was impossible to know these people, nor did they sometimes, as I have said, know themselves to be infected." p. 220.

(c) "[People apparently well often had the contagion] really upon them, and in their blood, yet did not show the consequences of it in their countenances; nay even were not sensible of it themselves." *Ib.*

(d) "And this is the reason why it is impossible in a visitation to prevent the spreading of the plague by the utmost human vigilance, viz., that it is impossible to know the infected people from the sound, or that the infected people should perfectly know themselves." *Ib.*

(e) "The plague is not to be avoided by those that converse promiscuously in a town infected, and people have it when they know it not, and they likewise give it to others when they know not they have it themselves." p. 221.

(f) "Shutting up the well or removing the sick will not [prevent the spread of the distemper] unless they can go back and shut up all those that the sick had conversed with, even before they knew themselves to be sick . . . for none knows when, or where, or how they have received the infection, or from whom." *Ib.*

(g) "One man who may really have received the infection and knows it not, but goes abroad and about as a sound person, may give the plague to a thousand

---

[85] The paging refers to "Everyman's Library," which, by the way, classes the "Journal" as "fiction."

people, ... and neither the person giving the infection or the person receiving it know anything of it, and perhaps feel the effects of it for several days after [when the tokens would appear] ... and yet, as I said, they knew nothing of their being infected, nor found themselves as much as out of order, till those mortal marks were upon them." p. 225.

(h) "Men went about apparently well many days after they had the taint of the disease in their vitals, and after their spirits were so seized as that they never could escape it, and that all the while they did so they were dangerous to others." p. 229.

(i) "Fathers and mothers have gone about as if they had been well, and have believed themselves to be so, till they have insensibly infected and been the destruction of their whole families." p. 232.

(j) "Many people having been well to the best of their own judgment, ... for several days, ... have been found ... at the brink of death, ... and a walking destroyer perhaps for a week or a fortnight before that." *Ib*.

(k) "The schemes [for shutting up infected houses] cannot take place but upon those that appear to be sick, or to be infected; whereas there are among them at the same time thousands of people who seem to be well, but are all the while carrying death with them into all companies which they come into." p. 233.

(l) "The apothecaries and surgeons knew ... that many people had the plague in their very blood, ... and were in themselves walking putrefied carcasses, ... and yet were as well to look on as other people, and even knew it not themselves." *Ib*.

(m) "The infection is retained in bodies apparently well, and conveyed from them to those they converse with, while it is known to neither the one nor the other." p. 238.

(n) "When people began to be convinced that the infection was received in this surprising manner from persons apparently well, they began to be exceedingly shy of every one that came near them." *Ib*.

(o) "I observed that after people were possessed, as I have said, with the belief, or rather assurance, of the infection being thus carried on by persons apparently in health, the churches and meeting-houses were much thinner of people than at other times before that they used to be." p. 239.

(p) "When the physicians assured us that the danger was as well from the sound as the sick, and that those people who thought themselves entirely free were oftentimes the most fatal; . . . then, I say, they began to be jealous of everybody." p. 240.

The foregoing extracts do not include several stories growing out of, or corollaries to, the statements of fact respecting the unconscious spreading of the distemper. Indeed, these are really not stories, but merely further repetitions of the known facts. It is this method of stating a fact as an experience of the narrator that has caused deception concerning the real nature of the *Journal*, and has served to cover up many of the repetitions. Concerning these repetitions, it is doubtful whether, without the minutest analysis, any but the most careful student of Defoe would ever dream of the wanton number he indulges in. A very close examination of the *Journal* discloses how skilfully he has covered up both the padding and the method of its accomplishment, by distributing his materials, rearranging and recombining them in slightly altered garbs, as the statement of facts in the semblance of stories. A still closer examination of Defoe's methods reveals the fact that when he takes his starting point for his repetitions from a given source, he repeats practically all that he has taken from that author. As his various sources emphasize different characteristics of the Plague, it is easy for the ordinary reader to believe that Defoe, though repeating to an extent, is constantly presenting new facts, new conditions, new aspects, new stories. Thus, the series of repetitions within repetitions serve to a large degree to conceal the process itself. It is doubtful whether Defoe was conscious of this, but, at any rate, it is his most striking accomplishment in writing the *Journal*.

Closely allied to, and abetting, this process of hiding endless repetitions in the *Journal*, is the digressionary method (or lack of method) which so frequently appears. Defoe began his history in a straightforward manner, copying directly from his printed sources. But he had not gone far until he saw that he must run dry before he had half a book. He therefore began to embroider upon his facts by circling round and round them, digressing and repeating, one time picking up an item here to start from, another time an item from another source, etc. After printing the "Orders conceived by the Lord Mayor," this digressionary and circling process begins. It is relieved by an occasional injection of figures from the

Bills, and illustrative stories, extracts from the newspapers regarding trade, etc., but, in the main, the genuine additions to the history of the Plague, after the first third of the *Journal* is past, are really very few until we come to near the close of the book, and even here we find much that has been recorded in earlier pages. No better example of the befogging effect of Defoe's digressions can be found than in the manner in which he introduces his story of the sailor, soldier, and joiner. He first begins the story rather early in the *Journal*, but immediately rambles off to the great pit, wickedness of the buriers, cruelty of nurses, blasphemous tipplers, and church-going. Then he gets back to blasphemy again, thence to shutting up of houses, violence of watchmen, spreading of the Plague by the diseased victims breaking out, observations on the cause of spreading the distemper, dismal street scenes, and private meditations! It now occurs to him to introduce Dr. Heath, but he is immediately forced back to the cause of the spread of the Plague—as if he had not already discussed it several times—then more dismal street scenes, how the inhabitants managed to get their provisions, more melancholy stories, cruel nurses and robbery stories repeated, and so on, and so on, for over seventy pages. Then he bethought him of the three men who escaped to the country; but at once breaks off again and discusses the order for killing dogs and cats. Finally, however, "I come back to my three men," whom he sticks pretty close to for about eight pages; then he drops them for a couple of pages to follow the progress of the Plague about Wapping, Ratcliff, etc., at last

"to return to my travellers," which he does rather
consistently, and concludes his story with only one
further digression. After throwing in this rather
long-drawn-out story in the methodless fashion I have
described, Defoe could return to his repetitions with
less chance of detection. It is altogether likely,
however, that deception, in this respect, formed no part
of Defoe's intent, that the haphazard result was a genuine Topsy case.

IV

From the foregoing thesis and from the appendices to this discussion, it is abundantly evident that Defoe's *Journal of the Plague Year* is a faithful record of historical facts, that it was so intended by the author and is as nearly correct as it was humanly possible to make it from the sources and time at his command. Such errors—few in number and slight in importance—as crept in, arose from faulty and confused sources, or from haste, and are in no wise attributable to bias on the one hand, or to imagination or style on the other. An analysis of the sources and facts available to Defoe, and a comparison of these to unpublished letters and other documents inaccessible to him, prove the soundness of this conclusion. There is not one single statement in the *Journal*, pertinent to the history of the Great Plague in London, that has not been verified during the course of this investigation, even to the stories related by Defoe, the originals of which, or parallels, have been discovered.

From what I have written concerning the sources of the *Journal*, it is clear that these are of two kinds. In the first place, there are the printed accounts of the Plague found in Hodges's *Loimologia*, Kemp's *Brief Treatise*, Vincent's *God's Terrible Voice in the City*, Thomson's *Loimotomia*, in *Golgotha*, and numerous other contemporaneous accounts of the Plague of 1665; not to mention historical accounts of earlier plagues in other countries, as those of Thucydides,

Baccaccio, Diemerbroick, etc., and those of Defoe's contemporaries, Mead, Pye, Quincy, Chicoyneau, and others. From these he got not only the facts concerning the origin, symptoms, and treatment of the distemper, but also the effects of the calamity on trade, on the appearance of the town and on the spirits of the people, as well as many illustrative stories. The newspapers of the times furnished him with the weekly Bills of Mortality, the progress of the contagion, weather conditions, movements of the Court, proclamations regarding fasts, inhibitions of fairs in various parts of the kingdom, the building of fires in the streets in an attempt to check the spread of the disease, orders and prescriptions of the College of Physicians, the activities of the Mayor and Aldermen, advertisements of the quacks, the lists of charitable contributions the alarms raised by the comets of 1664, together with the numerous interpretations of their meaning, accounts of other prodigies, stories about victims of the Plague, etc., etc. The newspapers were a perfect mine of plague materials. The Bills of Mortality, prepared by the Parish Clerks, were also available in print as well as *A Collection of Very Valuable and Scarce Pieces Relating to the Plague*. This last was much used by Defoe. Almanacks and other printed prognostications and predictions were only too numerous.

A second fruitful source that Defoe drew upon in writing his *Journal of the Plague* was his own memory of the eventful happenings of 1665, and especially the many stories related to him by the survivors of the Plague. By survivors, I do not mean simply those who were still alive in 1722 (of whom there must have been many), but also those who lived ten, or even five, years after 1665, when Defoe was at the greatest impressionable age to retain and appreciate the awfulness of the calamity. Thus, for instance, there is no anachronic reason why Defoe should not have known personally—and in some cases for years—nearly every one of the authors of the printed sources mentioned in the course of this discussion. Of course there were scores of other survivors of the Plague from whom he could have heard the various stories which he relates. Besides, it is not to be forgotten that a disaster of such magnitude was no nine-days wonder; it must have furnished the topic for the evening fireside for many a year after the event. All of this was revivified and retold when the news of the Marseilles Plague reached England. Doubtless, many of Defoe's stories were first-hand; and, anyhow, it was unnecessary for him to invent any of them,—nothing could surpass the real facts, whether they were wanted for fiction or for history.

Of the two kinds of materials used in making up the *Journal*, the printed are of chief importance. As I have already shown, these form not only the framework of the book but also the bulk of it: if it were divested of all other features, we would still have left an authentic history of the Plague, as fully demonstrated in section two of this essay. Defoe transcribes the facts without alteration or equivocation. Occasionally, when some mere theory (as of the efficacy of fires in the street, shutting-up, or other treatment of the contagion, is under discussion, he expresses an opinion, a liberty granted to all historians; but even in such case, Defoe offers nothing new beyond his sources, the arguments which he adduces are to be found there. As for the hearsay stories and traditions which he repeats, there is no reason to doubt their authenticity; there are many substantiating parallels. The fact is, Defoe was over-scrupulous in regard to these, often declining to vouch for them. As already pointed out, this has been a chief cause for classing the *Journal* with fiction. In the first part of this investigation appears a sufficient number of originals, prototypes, and parallels to the stories in the *Journal* to justify their being classed as historical. All historical students know that two perfectly authentic histories may be written from incidents and materials differing slightly in externals but bearing internal resemblances that are unmistakable. More fully to illustrate this fact, I have quoted not only from sources with which Defoe was most certainly acquainted, but also I have drawn from books and manuscripts of which he could not have known. The results, to all intents and purposes, are identical, and for this reason we are compelled to class the *Journal of the Plague Year* with authentic histories.

APPENDIX A.

From NATHANIEL HODGES'S *Loimologia: or, An Historical Account of the Plague in London in 1665: with precautionary Directions against the like Contagion.* JOHN QUINCY, M. D., TRANS.
1720.

The Plague which we are now to give an account of, discovered the beginnings of its future cruelties about the close of the year 1664; for at that season two or three persons died suddenly in one family in Westminster, attended with like symptoms, that manifestly declared their origin: hereupon some timorous neighbours, under apprehension of a contagion, removed into the city of London, who unfortunately carried along with them the pestilential taint; whereby that disease which before was in its infancy, in a family or two, suddenly got strength and spread abroad its fatal poison; and merely for want of confining the persons first seized with it, the whole city was in a little time irrecoverably infected. Not unlike what happened the year following, when a small spark, from an unknown cause, for want of timely care, increased to such a flame that neither tears of the people nor the profusion of their Thames could extinguish; and which laid waste the greatest part of the City in three days time: and therefore as there happens to be no great difference between these two grievous calamities, this mention of them together may not be improper; and the more especially, because by a like irresistible fate from a fever and a conflagration, both the inhabitants and their houses were reduced to ashes.

But as soon as it was rumoured amongst the common people, who are always enough astonished at any thing new, that the Plague was in the city, it is impossible to relate what accounts were spread of its fatality, and well were it had not the presages been so ominous; every one predicted its future devastation, and they terrified each other with remembrances of a former pestilence; for it was a received notion amongst the common people, that the Plague visited England once in twenty years; as if after a certain interval, by some inevitable necessity, it must return again. But although this conceit, how well soever justified by past experience, did not so much obtain with persons of more judgment, yet this may be affirmed, that it greatly contributed, amongst the populace, both to propagate and inflame the contagion, by the strong impressions it made upon their minds.

And these frightful apprehensions were not a little increased by the predictions of astrologers, from the conjunctions of stars, and the appearances of comets; for although but little regard was given to such things by persons of thought, yet experience duly showed what influence they had with the meaner sort whose spirits being manifestly sunk by such fears, rendered their constitutions less able to resist the contagion. Whosoever duly considers it, can never imagine that this pestilence had its origin from any conjunction of Saturn and Jupiter in Sagitarius on the tenth of October, or from a conjunction of Saturn and Mars in the same sign on the twelfth of November, which was the common opinion; for all the good that happens during the like conjunctions is assignable to the same causes.

The like judgment is to be made of comets, how terrible soever they may be in their aspects, and whether they are produced in the higher regions from a conglomeration of many stars, and returning at certain periods; or whether they are lower, and the production of sulphurous exhalations, kindled in our own atmosphere; for there is nothing strange in the ascension of heterogeneous particles into a flame, upon their rapid occursions and collisions against each other, howsoever terrible the track of such light may be circumstanced. The people therefore were frightened without reason at such things, and the mischief was much more in the predictions of the star-gazers than in the stars themselves: nothing however could conquer their sad impressions, so powerful were they amongst the populace who anticipated their unhappy fate with their fears, and precipitated their own destruction.

But to pass by things of less moment, it is to be taken notice that a very hard frost set in in December, which continued three months, and seemed greatly to deaden the contagion, and very few died during that season; although even then it was not extinguished, for in the middle of Christmas holidays, I was called to a young man in a fever, who after two days course of alexiterial medicines, had two risings about the bigness of a nutmeg broke out, one on each thigh; upon examination of which, I soon discovered the malignity, both from their black hue, and the circle round them, and pronounced it to be the plague; in which opinion I was afterwards confirmed by subsequent symptoms, although by God's blessing the patient recovered.

This case I insert, both to show that this season did not wholly destroy the distemper, although it greatly restrained it; but upon the frost breaking, the contagion got ground, and gradually got out of its confinements; like a flame that for some time seems smothered, and suddenly breaks out with aggravated fury.

As soon as the magistracy, to whom belonged the public care, saw how the contagion daily increased, and had now extended itself to several parishes, an order was immediately issued out to shut up all the infected houses, that neither relations nor acquaintance might unwarily receive it from them, and to keep the infected from carrying it about with them.

But whether this method proved of service or not, is to this day doubtful, and much disputed; but it is my business here however to adhere to facts, and relate the arguments on both sides with all possible impartiality.

In order whereunto, it is to be observed, that a law was made for marking the houses of infected persons with a

red cross, having with it this subscription, LORD HAVE
MERCY UPON US: and that a guard should there continually attend both to hand to the sick the necessaries of food
and medicine, and to restrain them from coming abroad
until forty days after their recovery. But although the
Lord Mayor and all inferior officers readily and effectually
put these orders in execution, yet it was to no purpose, for
the plague more and more increased; and the consternation
of those who were separated from all society, unless with
the infected, was inexpressible; and the dismal apprehension it laid them under, made them but an easier prey to
the devouring enemy. And this seclusion was on this account much the more intolerable, that if a fresh person
was seized in the same house but the day before another
had finished the quarantine, it was to be performed over
again; which occasioned such tedious confinements of sick
and well together that some times caused the loss of the
whole.

But what greatly contributed to the loss of people
thus shut up, was the wicked practices of nurses (for they
are not to be mentioned but in the most bitter terms):
these wretches, out of greediness to plunder the dead,
would strangle their patients, and charge it to the distemper in their throats; others would secretly convey the
pestilential taint from sores of the infected to those who
were well; and nothing indeed deterred these abandoned
miscreants from prosecuting their avaricious purposes by
all the methods their wickedness could invent; who, although they were without witness to accuse them, yet it is
not doubted but divine vengeance will overtake such wicked
barbarities with due punishment: nay, some were remarkably struck from heaven in the perpetration of their
crimes, and one particularly amongst many, as she was
leaving the house of a family, all dead, loaded with her
robberies, fell down dead under her burden in the streets:
and the case of a worthy citizen was very remarkable, who
being suspected dying by his nurse, was beforehand stripped
by her; but recovering again, he came a second time into

[104]

the world naked. And so many were the artifices of these barbarous wretches, that it is to be hoped posterity will take warning how they trust them again in like cases; and that their past impunities will not be a means of bringing on us again the like judgment.

Moreover, this shutting up infected houses, made the neighbours fly from theirs, who otherwise might have been a help to them on many accounts; and I verily believe that many who were lost might have now been alive, had not the tragical mark upon their door drove proper assistance from them.

And this is confirmed by the examples of other pestilential contagions, which have been observed not to cease until the doors of the sick were set open, and they had the privilege of going abroad; of the same authority is the custom of other nations who have due regard to that liberty that is necessary for the comforts of both body and mind.

It now remains that we take notice of all that is of any weight on the other side; as therefore it is not at all deemed cruel to take off a mortified limb to save the whole, by a parity of reason is the conduct of a community justifiable, who, out of a regard to the public good, put hardships upon particular persons; in a pestilential contagion therefore, what can be of more immediate service than securing those that are well from the infection? And the more especially in a disease that reaches not only the body, but taints the very breath; for in this case the infected breathe poisons upon the healthful, and even at the point of death endeavors to infuse that venom to others that conquered them. From this delirious pleasure arises those tricks of transplanting the corruption of a pestilential tumour to another; not to say anything of that woman, who with her importunities drew her unhappy husband into her embraces, which ended his life with hers.

Again, to take away all doubtings in this case, I am not ignorant of what moment it is to shut up the houses of all those who are infected, according to custom; for by this means a contagion may at first be stifled, which otherwise would go beyond any remedy; and with equal advantage might gunpowder be fired, if too much time is not wasted in deliberation, before these things are put into practice.

But if hereafter again a plague should break out (which God forbid), with submission to superiors, I should think it not improper to appoint proper accommodations out of the city, for such as are yet untouched in infected families; and who should continue there for a certain time; the sick in the meantime to be removed to convenient apartments provided on purpose for them. For by this means, that practice so abhorrent to religion and humanity, even in the opinion of a Mahometan, of shutting up the sick and well together, would be avoided.

But to return: the infection had long doubtfully reigned, and continued through May and June, with more or less severity; sometimes raging in one part, and then in another, as in a running sort of fight; as often as the number of funerals decreased, great hopes were conceived of its disappearance; then on a sudden again their increase threw all in dejection, as if the whole city was soon to be unpeopled — which uncertainty gave advantage to the distemper; because persons were more remiss in their provisions against it, during such fluctuation.

It must not however be omitted, with what precipitation the trembling inhabitants left the city, and how they flocked in such crowds out of town, as if London had quite gone out of itself, like the hurry of a sudden conflagration, all doors and passages are thronged for escape: yet after the chief of the people were fled, and thereby the nourishment of this cruel enemy had been in a great measure taken away, yet it raged still; and although it seemed once to slay as Parthians in their flight, it soon returned with redoubled fury, and killed not by slow paces, but almost immediately upon seizure; not unlike what is often seen in battle, when after some skirmishes of wings, and separate parties, the main bodies come to engage; so did this contagion at first only scatter about its arrows, but at last covered the whole city with dead.

Thus therefore in the space of one week were eighty persons cut off, and when things came to extremity, all helps were called in; though it began now to be solely the magistrates' business, how to put a stop to this cruel devastation, and save some part of the city at last from the grave; first then therefore were appointed a monthly fast for public prayers, to deprecate the anger of heaven; nor proved it in vain, or were their supplications altogether fruitless; for if we have any regard to the temperature of the season, the whole summer was refreshed with moderate breezes, sufficient to prevent the air's stagnation and corruption, and to carry off the pestilential streams; the heat was likewise too mild to encourage such corruption and fermentation as helps to taint the animal fluids, and prevent them from their natural state.

The Government, however, to the duty of public prayers, neglected not to add what assistance might be had from medicines; to which purpose His Majesty, with the Divine helps, called in also all that was human, and by his Royal authority commanded the College of Physicians of London jointly to write somewhat in English that might be a general directory in this calamitous exigence. Nor was it satisfactory to that honoured Society to discharge their regards for the public with that only, but some were chose out of their number, and appointed particularly to attend the infected on all occasions; two also out of the court of Aldermen were required to see this hazardous task executed; so that encouraged with all proper means, this province was cheerfully undertaken, and all possible caution was used fully to answer the intention; but this task was too much for four persons, and wanted rather the concurrence of the whole Faculty; we were however ashamed to give it up, and used our utmost application therein; but all our care and pains were eluded, for the disease, like the hydra's heads, was no sooner extinguished in one family, but it broke out in many more with aggravations, so that in a little time we found our task too great, and despaired of putting an entire stop to the infection.

Nor was there at this time wanting the help of very great and worthy persons who voluntarily contributed their assistances in this dangerous work; amongst the number of which the learned Dr. Glisson, Regius Professor at Cambridge, Dr. Nath. Paget, Dr. Wharton, Dr. Berwick, Dr. Brookes, and many others who are yet alive, deserve very honourable mention; but eight or nine fell in this work, who were too much loaded with the spoils of the enemy; and amongst these was Dr. Conyers whose goodness and humanity claim an honourable remembrance with all who survive him.

After then all endeavours to restrain the contagion proved of no effect, we applied ourselves to the care of the diseased; and in the prosecution of which, it may be affirmed without boasting, no hazards to ourselves were avoided. But it is incredible to think how the plague raged amongst the common people, insomuch that it came by some to be called "the poor's plague." Yet, although the more opulent had left the town, and that it was almost left uninhabited, the commonality that were left felt little of want; for their necessities were relieved with a profusion of good things from the wealthy, and their poverty was supported with plenty. A more manifest cause therefore for such a devastation amongst them I shall assign in another place.

In the months of August and September, the contagion changed its former slow and languid pace, and having as it were got master of all, made a most terrible slaughter, so that three, four, or five thousand died in a week, and once eight thousand. Who can express the calamities of such times? The whole British nation wept for the miseries of her metropolis. In some houses carcasses lay waiting for burial, and in others persons in their last agonies; in one room might be heard dying groans, in another the raving of delirium, and not far off relations and friends bewailing both their loss and the dismal prospect of their own sudden departure. Death was the sure midwife to all children, and infants passed immediately from the womb to the grave. Who would not burst with grief to see the stock for a future generation hanging upon the breasts of a dead mother? Or the marriage-bed changed the first night into a sepulchre, and the unhappy pair meet with death in their first embraces? Some of the infected ran about staggering like drunken men, and fell and expired in the streets; while others lie half-dead and comatose, but never to be waked but by the last trumpet; some lie vomiting as if they had drunk poison; and others fell dead in the market, while they were buying necessaries for the support of life. Not much unlike was it in the following conflagration, where altars themselves became so many victims, and the finest churches in the whole world carried up to heaven supplications in flames, while their marble pillars wet with tears melted like wax; nor were monuments secure from the inexorable flames, where many of their venerable remains passed a second martyrdom; the most august palaces were soon laid waste, and the flames seemed to be in a fatal engagement to destroy the great ornament to commerce; and the burning of all the commodities of the world together seemed a proper epitome of this conflagration; neither confederate crowns nor the drawn swords of kings could restrain its phanatic and rebellious rage; large halls, stately houses, and the sheds of the poor were together reduced to ashes; the sun blushed to see himself set, and envied those flames the government of the night, which had rivalled him so many days. As the city, I say, was afterwards burnt without any distinction, in like manner did this plague spare no order, age, or sex. The divine was taken in the very exercise of his priestly office to be enrolled amongst the saints above; and some physicians, as before intimated, could not find assistance in their own antidotes, but died in the administration of them to others; and although the soldiery retreated from the field of death, and encamped out of the city, the contagion followed and vanquished them. Many in their old age, others in their prime, sunk under its cruelties. Of the female sex most died; and hardly any children escaped; and it was not uncommon to see an inheritance pass successively to three or four heirs in as many days. The number of sextons was not sufficient to bury the dead; the bells seemed hoarse with continual tolling, until at last they quite ceased; the burying places would not hold the dead, but they were thrown into large pits dug in waste grounds, in heaps, thirty or forty together; and it often happened that those who tended the funerals of their friends one evening were carried the next to their long home.

> . . . *Quis talia fundo*
> *Temperet a lachrymis?*

Even the relation of this calamity melts me into tears. And yet the worst was not certain, although the city was near drained by her funerals, for the disease as yet had no relaxation.

About the beginning of September, the disease was at its height; in the course of which month more than twelve thousand died in a week. But at length, that nothing might go untried to divert the contagion, it was ordered by the governors who were left to superintend those calamitous affairs (for the Court was then removed to Oxford), to burn fires in the streets for three days together; yet while this was in debate, the physicians concerned were diffident of the success, as the air in itself was uninfected, and therefore rendered such a showy and expensive a project superfluous and of no effect; and these conjectures we supported by the authority of antiquity, and Hippocrates himself; notwithstanding which, the fires were kindled in all the streets. But alas! the controversy was soon decided, for before the three days were quite expired the heavens both mourned so many funerals, and wept for the fatal mistake, so as to extinguish even the fires with their showers. I shall not determine any other person's conjecture in this case, whether these fires may more properly be deemed the ominous forerunners of the ensuing conflagrations, or the ensuing funerals; but whether it was from the suffocating qualities of the fuel, or the wet constitution of the air that immediately followed, the most fatal night ensued wherein more than four thousand perished. May posterity by this mistake be warned, and not, like empirics, apply a remedy where they are ignorant of the cause.

The reader is by the way to be advertised that the year was luxuriant in most fruits, especially cherries and grapes which were at so low a price that the common people surfeited with them; for this might very much contribute to the disposition of the body, as made this pestilential taint more easily take place.

Nor ought we here to pass by the beneficent assistance of the rich, and the care of the magistrates; for the markets being open as usual, and a great plenty of all provisions was a great help to support the sick, so that there was the reverse of a famine which hath been observed to be so fatal to pestilential contagions; and in this the goodness of heaven is always to be remembered, in alleviating a common misery by such a provision of good things from the stores of nature.

But as it were to balance this immediate help of Providence, nothing was otherwise wanting to aggravate the common destruction, and to which nothing more contributed than the practice of chymists and quacks, and of whose audacity and ignorance it is impossible to be altogether silent. They were indefatigable in spreading their antidotes; and although equal strangers to all learning as well as physic, they thrust into every hand some trash or other under the disguise of a pompous title. No country, surely, ever abounded with such wicked impostors; for all events contradicted their pretensions, and hardly a person escaped that trusted to their delusions. Their medicines were more fatal than the plague, and added to the numbers of the dead. But these blowers of the pestilential flame were caught in the common ruin, and by their death in some measure excused the neglect of the magistrates in suffering their practice.

[111]

. . . Nec lex est justior ulla
Quam necis artifices arte perire sua.

About this time a person of distinction and great humanity, going to France upon some affairs of State, heard that some Frenchmen were masters of the anti-pestilential remedy, and took care to send some doses of it over here. By command of the Government we were ordered to try it with due caution, which we did with expectations of uncommon success; but the mountain brought forth death, for the medicine, which was a mineral preparation, threw the patients into their last sleep. May it never hereafter be enjoined to try experiments with unknown and foreign medicines upon the lives even of the meanest persons! For certainly nothing is more abhorrent to reason than to impose a universal remedy in cases whose curative intentions are different and sometimes opposite; and the various indications of pestilence require very different methods of remedy, as shall hereafter be further demonstrated [in the Section dealing with the "Cure of the Pestilence"].

To this may be added that many common medicines were publicly sold, which by their extraordinary heat and disposition to inflame the blood could never be fit for every age, sex, and constitution indifferently, and therefore in many cases must undoubtedly do harm. On this account not only the sacred art, but the public health also, suffered; yet we who were particularly employed in this affair as physicians, used all solicitations with the magistracy to restrain such practices in order to stop the ruin they aggravated. Hence, notwithstanding it was made a question whether in a plague, where so many physicians retire (not so much for their own preservation as the service of those whom they attend), it is not expedient for every one, according to his abilities, to do his utmost in averting a common ruin? In the same manner as in a fire all hands are required, even of the crowd as well as workmen, to extinguish it.

But in this case my own opinion is determined: in the restoration of health, a person must proceed with more caution and deliberation than in the supposed case of a fire; for there are difficulties occur in the practice of medicine which are insuperable but by the unlearned; and the fine texture of a human body is not to be managed by as clumsy hands as the materials of a house; in the former, if a person makes a mistake, it is with great difficulty repaired; and, therefore, upon a serious consideration of the whole affair, I cannot make any doubt, but it is much better to want physicians in such calamities, than to have the sick under the care and management of the unlearned; for such persons, like those who fight blindfold, know not in what parts to attack the enemy, nor with what weapons to do it; besides which, they are also in hazard of obstructing these efforts of nature, which would many times without help, if not thus hindered, get the better of the distemper.

Nor in this account are we to neglect, that the contagion spread its cruelties into the neighbouring countries; for the citizens, which crowded in multitudes into the adjacent towns, carried the infection along with them, where it raged with equal fury; so that the plague, which at first crept from one street to another, now reigned over whole counties, leaving hardly any place free from its insults; and the towns upon the Thames were more severely handled, not perhaps from a great moisture in the air from thence, but from the tainted goods rather that were carried up it. Moreover, some cities and towns of the most advantageous situation for a wholesome air, did notwithstanding feel the common ruin. Such was the rise and such the progress of this cruel destroyer which first began at London.

But the worst part of the year being now over, and the height of the disease, the plague by leisurely degrees declined, as it had gradually made its first advances; and before the number infected decreased, its malignity began to relax, insomuch that few died, and those chiefly such as were ill managed. Hereupon that dread which had been upon the minds of the people wore off; and the sick cheerfully used all the means directed for their recovery; and even the nurses grew either more cautious or more faithful; insomuch that after some time a dawn of health appeared as sudden and as unexpected as the cessation of the following conflagration, wherein after blowing up of houses, and using all means for its extinction to little purpose, the flames stopped as it were of themselves, for want of fuel or out of shame for having devoured so much.

The pestilence however did not stop for want of subjects to act upon (as then commonly rumoured), but from the nature of the distemper its decrease was like its beginning, moderate; nor is it less to be wondered at that as at the rise of the contagion all other distempers went into that, so now at its declension that degenerated into others, as inflammations, headaches, quinsies, dysenteries, smallpox, measles, fevers, and hectics; wherein that also yet predominated, as hereafter will be further shown [in the Section on "The Signs of the late Pestilence"].

About the close of the year, that is, on the beginning of November, people grew more healthful, and such a different face was put upon the public, that although the funerals were yet frequent, yet many who had made most haste in retiring, made the most to return, and came into the city without fear; insomuch that in December they crowded back as thick as they fled. The houses which before were so full of the dead, were inhabited now by the living, and the shops which had been most part of the year shut up were again opened, and the people again cheerfully went about their wonted affairs of trade and employ; and even, what is almost beyond belief, those citizens who before were afraid of their friends and relations, would without fear enter the houses and rooms where infected persons had but a little while before breathed their last. Nay, such comforts did inspire the languishing people, and confidence, that many went into the beds where persons had died, before they were even cold or cleansed from the stench of the diseased. They had the courage now to marry again, and betake to the means of repairing the past mortality; and even women before deemed barren were said to prove prolific, so that although the contagion had carried off, as some computed, about one hundred thousand, after a few months their loss was hardly discernible, and thus ended this fatal year.

But the next Spring, indeed, appeared some remains of the contagion, which was easily conquered by the physicians, and, like the termination of a common intermittent, ended in a healthful recovery; whereupon the whole malignity ceasing, the city returned to a perfect health; not unlike what happened also after the last conflagration, when a new city suddenly arose out of the ashes of the old, much better able to stand the like flames another time.

APPENDIX B.

FROM VINCENT'S *God's Terrible Voice in the City*, 1667.

It was in the year of our Lord 1665, that the Plague began in our City of *London*, after we were warned by the great Plague in *Holland*, in the year 1664, and the beginning of it in some remote parts of our Land in the same year; not to speak any thing whether there was any signification and influence in the *Blazing-Star* not long before, that appeared in the view of *London*, and struck some amazement upon the spirits of many: It was in the month of *May* that the Plague was first taken notice of; our Bill of Mortality did let us know of but three which died of the disease in the whole year before; but in the beginning of May the Bill tells us of nine, which fell by the Plague, one just in the heart of the City, the other eight in the Suburbs. This was the first arrow of warning that was shot from Heaven amongst us, and fear begins quickly to creep upon peoples hearts; great thoughts and discourse there is in Town about the Plague, and they cast in their minds whither they should go if the Plague should increase. Yet when the next weeks Bill signifieth to them the disease from 9 to 3, their minds are something appeased; discourse of this subject cools; fears are husht; and hope takes place, that the black cloud did but threaten, and give a few drops; but the wind would drive it away. But when in the next Bill the number of the dead by the Plague is amounted from 3 to 14, and in the next to 17, and in the next to 43, and the disease begins so much to increase and disperse, [fears are again aroused].

Now secure sinners begin to be startled, and those that would have slept at quiet still in their nests, are unwillingly awakened. Now a great consternation seizeth upon most persons, and fearful bodings of a desolating judgment. Now guilty sinners begin to look about them, and think with themselves into what corner of the Land they might fly to hide them. Now the prophane and sensual, if they have not remorse for their sins, yet dread and terrors, the effects of guilt, they could not drive from them; and if by company, and carousing, and soft pleasures they do intoxicate and smoothen their spirits in the day; yet we may guess what dread doth come upon them, if they give but any room for retirement, and what hideous thoughts such persons have in the silent night, through fears of death which they are in danger of. Now those who did not believe in any unseen God, are afraid of unseen arrows; and those which slighted Gods threatnings of eternal judgments, do tremble at his execution of one, and not the greatest temporal judgment. Now those which had as it were challenged the God of Heaven, and defied him by their horrid oaths and blasphemies, when he begins to appear, they retreat, yea fly away with terror and amazement. The great Orbs begin first to move; the Lords and Gentry retire into their Countries; their remote houses are prepared, goods removed, and *London* is quickly upon their backs: few truffling Gallants walk the streets: few spotted Ladies to be seen at windows: a great forsaking there was of the recent places where the Plague did first rage.

In *June* the number encreaseth from an 43 to 112; the next week to 168, the next to 267, the next to 470, most of which encrease was in the remote parts; few in this month within, or near the walls of the City; and few that had any note for goodness or profession, were visited at first; God gave them warning to think and prepare themselves; yet some few that were choice, were visited pretty soon, that the best might not promise to themselves a supercedeas, or interpret any place of Scripture so literally, as if the Lord had promised an absolute general immunity and defence of his own people from this disease of the Plague.

Now the Citizens of *London* are put to a stop in the career of their trade; they begin to fear whom they con-

verse withall, and deal withall, lest they should have come
out of infected places. Now Roses and other sweet Flowers
wither in the Garden, are disregarded in the Markets, and
people dare not offer them to their noses, lest with their
sweet savour, that which is infectious should be atracted:
Rue and *Wormwood* is taken into the hand; *Myrrhe* and
Zedoary are taken into the mouth; and without some antidote few stir abroad in the morning. Now many houses
are shut up where the Plague comes, and the inhabitants
shut in, lest coming abroad should spread infection. It
was very dismal to behold the Red Crosses, and read in
great letters *LORD HAVE MERCY UPON US,* on the
doors, and Watchmen standing before them with Halberts,
and such a solitude about those places, and people passing
by them so gingerly, and with such fearful looks, as if they
had been lined with enemies in ambush, and waited to
destroy them.

Now rich Tradesmen provide themselves to depart; if
they have not Countrey-houses, they seek Lodgings abroad
for themselves and Families, and the poorer Tradesmen,
that they may imitate the rich in their fear, stretch themselves to take a Countrey-journey, though they have scarce
wherewithall to bring them back again. The Ministers also
(many of them) take occasion to go to their Countrey-
places for the Summer-time; or (it may be) to find out
some few of their Parishioners that were gone before them,
leaving the greatest part of their Flock without food or
physick, in the time of their greatest need. (I don't speak
of all Ministers, those which did stay out of choice and
duty, deserve true honour). . . . I do not blame many
Citizens retiring, when there was so little trading, and
the presence of all might have help forward the encrease
and spreading of the Infection; but how did guilt drive
many away, where duty would have engaged them to stay
in the place? Now the highways are thronged with passengers and goods, and *London* doth empty itself into the
Countrey; great are the stirs and hurries in *London* by
the removal of so many families; fear puts many thousands

on the wing, and those think themselves most safe, that can flye furtherest off from the City.

In July the Plague encreaseth and prevaileth exceedingly, the number of 470 which dyes in one week by the disease, ariseth to 725 the next week, to 1089 the next, to 1843 the next, to 2010 the next. Now the Plague compasseth the Walls of the City like a flood, and poureth in upon it. Now most Parishes are infected both without and within: yea, there are not so many houses shut up by the Plague, as by the owners forsaking them for fear of it; and the Inhabitants be so exceedingly decreased by the departure of so many thousands, yet the number of dying persons encrease fearfully. Now the Countries keep guards, lest infectious persons from the City bring the Disease into them; most of the rich are now gone, and the middle sort will not stay behind; But the poor are forced (through poverty) to stay, and abide the storm. Now most faces gather paleness, and what dismal apprehensions do then fill their minds, what dreadful fears do there possess their spirits. . . , and the very sinking fears they have had of the Plague, hath brought the Plague and the death upon many; some by the sight of a Coffin in the streets, have fallen into a shivering, and immediately the death hath assaulted them, and clapt too the doors of their houses upon them, from whence they have come forth no more, till they have been brought forth to their graves; we may imagine the hideous thoughts, and horrid perplexity of mind, the tremblings, confusions, and anguish of spirit, which some awakened sinners have had, when the Plague hath broke in upon their houses, and seized upon near Relations, whose dying groans sounding in their ears have warned them to prepare; when their doors have been shut up, and fastned on the outside with an Inscription, *Lord have mercy upon us,* and none suffered to come in but a nurse, whom they have been more afraid of than the Plague itself; when Lovers and Friends, and Companions in sin have stood aloof, and not dared to come nigh the door of the house, lest death should issue forth from thence upon them, especially when the disease hath invaded themselves, and first began with a pain and diziness in their head, then trembling in their own members; when they have felt boiles to arise under their arms, and in their groins, and seen blains to come forth in other parts: when the disease hath wrought in them to that height, as to send forth those spots which (most think) are the certain Tokens of near approaching death; and now they have received the sentence of death within themselves, and have certainly concluded, that within a few hours they must go down into the dust, and their naked souls, without the case of their body, must make its passage into eternity, and appear before the Highest Majesty, to render their accounts, and receive their sentence: None can utter the horror which hath been upon the spirits of such, through the lashes and stings of their guilty consciences, when they have called to mind a life of sensuality, and profaneness, their uncleanness, drunkenness, injustice, oaths, curses, derision of Saints and holiness, neglect of their own salvation, and when a thousand sins have been set in order, before their eyes, with another aspect than when they looked upon them in the temptation. . . .

In *August* . . . the people fall as thick as leaves from the Trees in *Autumn* . . ., and there is a dismal solitude in *London-streets*. . . . Now shops are shut in, people rare and very few that walk about, insomuch that the grass begins to spring up in some places, and a deep silence almost in every place, especially within the Walls; no rattling Coaches, no prancing Horses, no calling in Customers, nor offering Wares, no *London Cryes* sounding in the ears; if any voice be heard it is the groans of dying persons, breathing forth their last; and the Funeral-knells of them that are ready to be carried to their Graves. Now shutting up of Visited-Houses (there being so many) is at an end, and most of the well are mingled among the sick, which otherwise would have got no help. Now in some places where the people did generally stay, not one house in an hundred but is infected, and in many houses half the

Family is swept away; in some the whole, . . . Now the nights are too short to bury the dead, the whole day (though at so great a length) is hardly sufficient to light the dead that fall therein, into their beds.

Now we could hardly go forth, but we should meet many Coffins, and see many with sores and limping in the streets; amongst other sad spectacles, methought two were very affecting; one of a woman coming alone, and weeping by the door where I lived (which was in the midst of the infection) with a little Coffin under her arm, carrying it to the new Church-yard: I did judg that it was the *mother of the child*, and that all the Family besides was dead, and she was forced to Coffin up, and bury with her own hands this her last dead child. Another, was of a man at the corner of the Artillery-wall, that as I judg through the diziness of his head with the disease, which seized upon him there, had dasht his face against the wall, and when I came by, he lay hanging with his bloody face over the rails, and bleeding upon the ground; and as I came back he was removed under a tree in *More-fields* and lay upon his back; I went and spake to him; he could make me no answer, but ratled in the throat, and as I was informed, within half an hour dyed in the place.

It would be endless to speak what we have seen and heard of some of their frensies, rising out of their beds and leaping about their rooms; others crying and roaring at their windows; some coming forth almost naked, and running into the streets; strange words have others spoken and done when the disease was upon them; But it was very sad to hear of one who being sick alone, and it is likely frantick, burnt himself in his bed. Now the Plague had broken in much amongst my acquaintance; and about sixteen or more whose faces I used to see every day in our house, within a little while I could find but four or six of them alive; scarcely a day passed over my head for I think a month or more together, but I should hear of the death of some one or more that I knew. . . .

In *September* the Grave doth open its mouth without measure. . . . The Church-yards now are stuft so full of dead corpses, that they are in many places swell'd two or three feet higher then they were before; and new ground is broken up to bury the dead.

.   .   .   .

Now some Ministers, formerly put out of their places, did abide in the City when most of Ministers in place were fled and gone from the people as well as the disease, into the Countreys, seeing the people crowd so fast into the grave and eternity, who seemed to cry as they went, for spiritual physicians; and perceiving that the Churches to be open, and the Pulpits to be open, and finding Pamphlets flung about the streets, of *Pulpits to be let,* they judged that the Law of God and Nature did now dispense with, yea command their Preaching in Publick places, though the Law of man . . . did forbid them to do it. . . .

Now there is such a vast concourse of people in the Churches where these Ministers are to be found, that they cannot many times come near the Pulpit-doors for the press, but are forced to clamber over the Pews to them: And such a face is now seen in the Assemblies, as seldom was seen before in *London,* such eager looks, such open ears, such greedy attention, as if every word would be eaten that dropt from the mouths of the Ministers. . . .

About the beginning of these Ministers preaching, especially after their first Fast together, the Lord begins to remit, and turn his hand, and cause some abatement of the disease.

.   .   .   .

Now the Citizens who had dispers'd themselves abroad into the Countries, because of the Contagion, think of their old Houses and Trades, and begin to return, though with fearfulness and trembling, lest some of the after drops of the storm should fall upon them: and O that many of them had not brought back their old hearts and sins, . . . Some return to their Houses and follow their worldly business, and work as hard as they can to fetch up the time they have lost, without minding and labouring to improve by the Judgment, and God's wonderful preservation of them, . . .

APPENDIX C

FROM BOGHURST'S *Loimographia*
1665, pr. 1894.

Almost all that caught this Disease with feare dyed with Tokens in two or three dayes.

About the beginning most men gott the disease with fadling, surfetting, overheating themselves, and disorderly living.

Tokens appeared not much till about the middle of June, and carbuncles not till the latter end of July, but were very rife in the Fall about September and October, and seized most on old people, adult, cholerick, and melancholy people, and generally on dry and leane bodyes. Children had none.

If very hott weather followed a shower of raine, the disease increased much.

If in the heate of the disease the winds blew very sharp and cold people dyed very quickly, many lying sicke but one day.

.   .   .   .

Shutting up of houses, wickedness, confident, ignorant mountebanks, overhasty cutting and burning sores, indulging too much to present ease, removeing servants and poore people to Pest-houses and to other houses in their sicknesse, overstifling and weakening people with too much sweating, overhasty going abroade into the cold, and preposterous Physick killed many.

.   .   .   .

Though all sorts of people dyed very thicke, both young and old, rich and poore, healthy and unhealthy, strong and weake, men and women of all constitutions, of all professions and places, of all religions, of all condi-

[124]

tions good and bad, yet as far as I could discerne the difference of the two, more of the good dyed then of the bad,
more men then women, and more of dulle complexions
then of faire.

. . . .

In the summer before the Plague in 1664 there was
such a multitude of flyes that they lined the insides of
houses, and if any threads or stringes did hang downe in
any place, it was presently thicke sett with flyes like a rope
of onions, and swarms of Ants covered the highways that
you might have taken up a handfull at a tyme, both winged
and creeping Ants; and such a multitude of croaking
froggs in ditches that you might have heard them before
you saw them. Also the same summer the Small Pox was
so rife in our Parish [of St. Giles in the Fields] that
betwixt the Church and the Pound in St. Giles, which is
not above six score paces, about forty familyes had the
Small Pox.

The Plague was ushered in with 7 months dry weather
and westerly windes.

. . . .

The Plague hath put itselfe forth in St. Giles's, St.
Clement's, St. Paul's, Covent Garden, and St. Martin's
this 3 or 4 yeares, as I have been certainly informed by
the people themselves that had it in their houses in these
Parishes.

The Plague first fell upon the highest ground, for our
Parish is the highest about London, and the best aire, yet
was first infected. Highgate, Hampstead, and Acton also
all shared in it.

. . . .

The winds blowing westward soe long together from
before Christmas until July, about 7 months, was the
cause the Plague began first at the West end of the City,
as at St. Giles's and St. Martin's Westminster. Afterwards
it gradually insinuated, and crept downe Holborne and the
Strand, and then into the City and at last to the East end
of the Suburbs; soe that it was half a yeare at the West
end of the City before the East end and Stepney was in-

fected, which was about the middle of July. Southwark being the South suburb, was infected almost as soon as the West end.

The Disease spread not altogether by contagion at first, nor began at only one place, and spread further and further as an eating spreading soare doth all over the body, but fell upon severall places of this City and Suburbs like raine, even at the first at St. Giles's, St. Martin's, Chancery Lane, Southwark, Houndsditch, and some places within the City, as at Proctor's House.

. . . . . .

This year in which the Plague hath raged soe much, noe alteration or change appeared in any element, vegetable or animall, besides the body of man, except only the season of the yeare and the windes, the spring being continuall dry for 6 or 7 months together, there being noe raine at all, but a little sprinkling Showre or two about the latter end of Aprill, which caused such a pitifull crop of Hay in the spring. Only in the Autumne there was a pretty good cropp, but all other things kept their common integrity, as all sorts of fruits, as Apples, Peares, Cherryes, Plums, Mulberryes, Raspes, Strawberryes; all roots as Parsnipps, Carrotts, Turnips; all flowers, all medicinable Simples, etc., were as plentifull, large, faire, and wholesome; all graine as plentifull and good; all kine, Cattle, Horses, Sheepe, Swine, Doggs, wild Beasts and tame, as healthfull, strong to labour, wholesome to eate as ever they were in any yeare. Though many pedling writers have undertaken to find fault with all these things, and made people so fearfull and carefull of what they eate or dranke, or what they bought, of keeping Doggs, of eating Mutton, Pork, Fish, Fruitts, Rootes, Salletts, especially cherryes, were much exclaimed at, and cucumbers. Yet I believe very few people eate soe much fruit continually as I did this yeare, yet was not once sicke of any disease all the yeare.

. . . . . .

I commonly drest forty soares in a day, held their pulse sweating in the bed half a quarter of an hour together to give judgement and informe myselfe in the various tricks of [the disease]: I lett one blood, gave glisters, though but to a few, held them up in their bedds to keep them from strangling and choking half an houre together, commonly suffered their breathing in my face severall tymes when they were dying, eate and dranke with them, especially those that had soares; sate downe by their bedd sides and upon their bedds discoursing with them an houre together if I had tyme, and stayd by them to see the manner of their death, and closed up their mouth and eyes (for they dyed with their mouth and eyes very much open and stareing); then if people had no body to helpe them (for helpe was scarce at such a tyme and place) I helpt to lay them forth out of the bedd and afterwards into the coffin, and last of all accompanying them to the grave.

APPENDIX D

From Kemp's *Brief Treatise*
1665.

[The *Plague*] sometimes begins with a cold shivering like
an Ague, sometimes continues with a mild warmth like Hec-
tick Fever or a Diary, and encreaseth with violent heat like
Burning Fever. It corrupteth the *Blood* and all the hu-
mours, it afflicteth the *Head* with pain, the *Brain* with gid-
diness, the *Nerves* with Convulsions, the *Eyes* with dimness,
making them look as if they had wept, and depriving them
of their lively splendor, it makes the *Countenance* look
ghastly, troubling the *Ears* with noise and deafness; it in-
fecteth the *Breath* with stinking, the *Voice* with hoarseness,
the *Throat* with soreness, the *Mouth* with drought, and the
Tongue with thirst; the *Stomach* with worms and want of
appetite, with hickhop, nauseousness, retching, and vomiting; the *Bowels* with looseness and the bloody Flix, the
Sides with stitches, the *Back* with pains, the *Lungs* with
flegme, the *Skin* with fainty and stinking Sweats, Spots,
Blains, Botches, Sores, and Carbuncles, the *Pulse* with
weakness, the *Heart* with sounding and faintness. It makes
feeble like the *Palsie,* it causes sleepiness like the *Lethargy,*
watchfulness and madness like a *Phrensie,* and sudden death
like the *Apoplexy.* And these symptomes happen not alike
to all.

. . . .

The Turks are perswaded, that every ones fate is written in his fore-head, and hath a fatal destiny appointed by
God . . .; by which credulity, they slight and neglect all care
of avoiding the infection, conversing with one another, and
buying the goods out of infected houses, and wearing the
apparel of them that lately died. . . . Multitudes have been
executed by the Plague for this Heresie. . . .

When the *Plague* begins to reign in any Place . . ., the Counsel of *Hypocrates* in advising to change and flye the corrupted air, is, and hath been received as an Oracle, . . . The Antidote made of three Adverbs, *Cito, Longe, Tarde, Flie quickly, Go far,* and *Return slowly,* hath oft-times proved effectual.

And if any of those that will strain at a Gnat, and swallow a Camel, should pretend any scruple of Conscience about the lawfulness of this Remedy, in *flying* from Infected Places, and say, out of envy, at the accommodation of others, or discontent that they are not so well provided themselves, or some secret design (as I have heard several express it) *The Lord can follow and find them out;* they may also understand, that it is not their desire to flie from his presence, but his Plague, not from their gracious God, but from his punishing and fearful rod. . . . But I shall leave these people as diseased in the Pate. . . .

But now if through Poverty and lack of means to maintain you, and want of friends to receive and entertain you in better air, or having such Callings, from the attendance whereon, you cannot with honesty and good conscience absent yourself, but are enforced still to stay . . ., you must then strengthen your Bodies against the Causes of the *Sicknesse.*

APPENDIX E

FROM *Golgotha, or a Looking-Glass for London,* 1665.

Let me suppose the case therefore to their [*i. e.* the College of Physicians'] consciences:

Whether, if four or five, or more of the skillfulest and hardiest of themselves, who have given this advice [to shut up infected houses] as Orthodox, against so many thousand poor Innocents, were to be coobed up in one of the poor houses, whereout but one dyed, and with them an old woman, or some ignorant creature (a stranger to them as is usual) for their Nurse, and a sturdy fellow without with an Halberd (or some stricter Watch, as they have advised for others) to have each of them no more than the Parish allows; and the Searchers, Chyrurgeons, &c. they have allowed to visit others, to visit them: if in a month or forty dayes after the last man of them dies, at such a season, so used, they do not think in their own consciences, with all their skill, their carcasses would all or most of them be carried away in the Night-Cart; which now (for fear thereof) are, many of them, got into their Country-Gardens, after their *Epistolary Vapour* and *Cruel Direction* aforesaid? How then may poor Women with child, Widows, helpless, friendless, Fatherless, and sucklings, exposed (without such help, as many have been) and half dead before, it may be by the sudden death of their first dead visited relation, escape the ruin of such further violence upon them?

Again, I query; If one in the Parish-Meeting-place fall suddenly sick or dye, after sitting there in the crowd two or three hours amongst the multitude; were it not as equal the doors should be shut upon the Assembly, or they in their several Houses shut up, as that some Families (who were further off from the single sick person that dyed therein) should be presently so violently used and exposed? O surely, if we would not be so done unto, these wayes then are unequal, and this violent course not like to abate our Plagues, but is rather a sign and earnest of further Wrath: And God (by leaving the Nation to be in love with such *unnatural Advice*) is, it's to be feared, paving a way for his Anger, in that more general shutting-up as a just Judgment on many accounts, prophesied of such a provoking City, *Isa.* 24, 10, 11, 12. *The City of confusion is broken down, every house is shut up,* &c.

3dly. It's full of evil effects, to the encrease of Plagues, and that not only as it provokes God as aforesaid, but naturally distracts men, filling them with horror of heart, but those that are shut-up, and those that live daily in the fear thereof; Most that are shut-up being surprized, unprovided, unsettled in house and heart, needing then most the use of a *sure friend, made for the day of adversity. Pro.* 17. 17. *An Interpreter* as *Elihu* speaks, *Job* 33. 23. *one of a thousand &c.* and are under soul-sinkings, and none to succour them; *their hearts die within them,* as *Nabals,* upon this bad news; not a friend to come nigh them in their many, many, heart and house cares and perplexities, compelled (though well) to lie by, or upon the death-bed (perhaps) of their dear relation, drag'd away before their eyes, affrighted children howling by their side, fitted by fainting affliction to receive the impression of a thousand fearful thoughts of the long night they have to reckon before release, after the last of the Family, so dismally exposed, shall sink by degrees, one after another, in the den of this dismal likeness to Hell, contrived by the Advice of the *English*-College of Doctors: no drop of water (perhaps) but what comes at the leisure of a drunken or careless Halberd-bearer at the door: no seasonable administration being as a certainty then for their support, and innumerable evils of this sort incident thereunto: whereof if the ear of any concerned were opened to the cry of the Poor herein, I could (upon knowledge) instance and give plentiful proof of one months misery and ruine already hereby upon many, enough to make the ears of every one that heareth tingle; and lay the blood of Innocents at the door of the Devisers and Prosecutors of this Barbarism; who also hereby bring no small consternation hourly upon the minds of those who are at liberty thoughtful (to terror) whose turn may be next to fall out of the oversight of their nearest Friends, into the hands of the Halberd, Searchers, and Chyrugion, all strangers to them, so as it may be plague enough to be haunted with, under such distraction and affliction. Hence (I say) are a thousand thoughts created, to such, swoondings, faintings, fears, (fitting for infection naturally) as have occasioned some already to lose their precious lives, and many have hardly escaped the effect thereof; who otherwise would not so dread the Visitation, that yet sink down and shiver now through fear hereof, but upon the sudden sight of a House shut-up, and clusters of little Children and tender ones in their windows, who might more rationally continue well by separation as they are able, or might be advised by a more charitable care of them, than by such miserable, noisome, melancholy, close imprisonment, which exposeth the *Well* (shut-up) daily to destruction, and also doth really but prepare a more unquenchable stench, and fest to wreak out of the windows (whilst so shut up) and disperse it self into the City by a more violent concourse to them at the window (though less to their relief) and by opening the doors (upon such choaking-up) for the Searchers and Bearers of the Dead (so daily more prepared for them) and other allowed Visitors, whose walks are far more perilous than twenty times so many left open to keep themselves clean and distant from the Sick and Dead, as else they would, to prevent their own infection.

Yea, after the House is allowed to be open, and all that are left alive are well after this usage, both they and it are far more Dangerous hereby to others, than before, they were crowded up so long to such a nasty and infecting station, being the natural and artificial way also hermetically to effect the most forceable and noisome putrifactions, when the *Embrio* shal be unsealed; common experience having proved it naturally less perilous to go to twenty visited kept sweet and clean, than to two so noisomly exposed.

To which I may add, that many for fear thereof do hide their Sores, and, (after a Sweat or two) their Sickness also, and go daily about their business so long as they can stand, mingled to much more danger every way: Nor dare any do the office of a Nurse or Friend to those shut-up (however necessary for the present distress) till help can be procured (whereby some have been neglected) because it is so penal, that they must be inclosed then themselves, how inconsistent soever to their charge and business, by which there comes no small inconveniency to the Sick, who are forced to take any ignorant Nurse (or worse) in haste, to their great hazard.

But lastly, I appeal to the experience of this and other parts; how apparently did the hand of the Lord rest (as the antient Citizens familiarly do observe) in the former great Plagues upon this City, when the people were wearied out of this oppression, under cause enough to mourn unto this day, over the cruelty every mercinary had opportunity to commit (as now) under colour hereof.

APPENDIX F

FROM *The Shutting up Infected Houses as it is practised in England Soberly Debated. By way of Address from the poor souls that are Visited to their Brethren that are Free.* 1665.

We [who are shut up] are acted by a Principle of self preservation, as well as you [who are fled and are free], and therefore as soon as we find ourselves or any member of our Families infected, so dradful is it to us to be shut up from all comfort and society, from free and wholsome air, from the care of the Physician, and the Divine, from the oversight of Friends and Relations, and sometimes even from the very necessities, and conveniences of Nature, that we run as far in City and Country as our feet can carry us, leaving Wives and Children to the Parishes, empty walls, and shops to Creditors, scattering the infection along the streets as we go, and shifting it from Lodging to Lodging with ourselves, till at last we drop in some Alley, Field, or neighbour Village, calling the people round about by the suddenness of our fall to stand awhile astonished at our deaths, and then take their own; each fearful man of us frighted from his own house, killing his whole Town by surprising them unprepared; whereas were we permitted to enjoy the content and freedom of our Habitations, we might by Antidotes, cure others, and be cured ourselves.

See, see, we infect not our next Neighbours, and this sickness spreads not much in any one place, but we carry it from place to place, running from our home as from our places of torment, and thus the Roads are visited, and men travel the same way to the Country, and to their long home: Thus the Contagion hath reached most places round the Citty, which is now as it were beseiged with the judgment, and encompassed with the Visitation and desolation: We have not learned how to manage a sickness, in all likelihood

[134]

did persons prepare themselves (upon the first breaking out of the Plague) with Antidotes to visit the sick, who would be very well contented to keep within doors, and converse only with their nearest Friends, (their Physicians and the ghostly fathers) and administer to them such preservatives, and other necessaries the Plague might go no further.

. . . .

This shutting up would breed a Plague if there were none: Infection may have killed its thousands, but shutting up hath killed its ten thousands. Little is it considered how careless most Nurses are in attending the Visited, and how careless (being possessed with rooking avarice) they are to watch their opportunity to ransack their houses; the assured absence of friends making the sick desperate on the one hand, and them on the other unfaithful: their estates are the Plague most dye on, if they have anything to lose, to be sure those are sad creatures (for the Nurses in such cases are the off-scouring of the City) have a dose to give them; besides that, it is something beyond a Plague to an ingenious spirit to be in the hands of those dirty, ugly, and unwholsome Haggs; even a hell it self, on the one hand to hear nothing but screetches, cryes, groans, and on the other hand to see nothing but ugliness and deformity, black as night, and dark as Melancholy: Ah! to lye at the mercy of a strange woman is sad: to leave wife, children, plate, jewels, to the ingenuity of poverty is worse; but who can express the misery of being exposed to their rapine that having nothing of the woman left but shape?

. . . . . .

For another Argument [against shutting up] I alledge the mischief and sad consequence that may arise from the high fits of Frenzy, that usually attend this and all other the like Distempers; wherein the sick (if not restrained by main force of their Attendants) are ready to commit any violence, either upon themselves or other, whether Wife, Mother, or Child. A sad instance whereof we had this last week in *Fleet* Lane, where the Man of the House being sick, and having a great Swelling, but not without hope of being almost ripe for breaking, did in a strong fit rise out of his bed, in spite of all that his Wife (who attended him) could do to the contrary, got his Knife, and therewith most miserably cut his Wife, and had killed her, had she not wrapped up the sheet about her, and therewith saved her self, till by crying out Murther, a Neighbour (who was himself shut up) opened his own doors, and forced into the house, and came seasonably to her preservation. The man is since dead, when in all likelihood (had he not by arising struck in the disease) he might have recovered.

Add to this a serious consideration of the sad condition of Women neer the time of their Travel, (or newly delivered) having neither Midwife to help them, nor Nurse to attend them, nor Necessaries provided for them, nor any friends to comfort them; and in this condition have continually for their object their own poor innocent Babes newly brought into the World, either to be starved for want of sustenance, or poysoned by the Breasts that should preserve them.

APPENDIX G

The season was admitted to be remarkably free from ordinary sickness; and if anybody was already ill of any other disease, it was absorbed in this. Many who were in perfect health, all in a moment, and without any apparent reason, were seized with violent heats in the head and with redness and inflamation of the eyes. Internally the throat and the tongue were quickly suffused with blood, and the breath became unnatural and fetid. There followed sneezing and hoarseness; in a short time the disorder, accompanied with a violent cough, reached the chest; then fastening lower down, it would move the stomach and bring on all the vomits of bile to which physicians have ever given names; and they were very distressing. An ineffectual retching producing violent convulsions attacked most of the sufferers; some as soon as the previous symptoms had abated, others not until long afterwards. The body externally was not so very hot to the touch, nor yet pale; it was of a livid colour inclining to red, and breaking out in pustules and ulcers. But the internal fever was intense; the sufferers could not bear to have on them even the finest linen garment; they insisted on being naked, and there was nothing which they longed for more eagerly than to throw themselves into cold water. . . . They could not sleep; a restlessness which was intolerable never left them. . . . Some escaped . . . [but] had no sooner recovered than they were seized with a forgetfulness of all things and knew neither themselves nor their friends. . . . Most appalling was the despondency which seized upon any one who felt himself sickening; for he instantly abandoned his mind to despair and, instead of holding out, absolutely threw away his chance of life. Appalling too was the rapidity with which they caught the infection; dying like sheep if they attended on one another; and this was the principal cause of mortality.

FROM *Harleian MSS*. 3,784 AND 3,785

Humphrey Henchman, Bishop of London, to Dr. William Sancroft, Dean of St. Paul's.

. . . .

The collection is to be for reliefe of persons and places visited with the sickness, the money to be gathered is to be sent in to the L. Maior for that vse: let the collection at S^{t:} Pauls be as it hath vsed to be vpon such occasions. J haue sent to my Register to disperse the Books, and to giue notice to the Ministers to exhort the people to this charity. J shall be at White Hall on Tuesday. I haue also written to m^{r.} Gifford to make such exhortation. J rest

Your very affectionate Brother

H. LONDON.

June 17 [1665]

To Reverend Doctor
  Sancroft Deane of
    St. Pauls
      London.

George Davenport to Dean Sancroft.

Aukland Castle, Jul. 1, 1665.

J am very sorry to hear ye sad relation you make about the Pestilence. Wee are in great fear, it will be brought from London to Newcastle.

Francis Wilson to Dean Sancroft.

Corp. Xti Coll Camb.

July 5, [1665].

S^r

We are now in that Condition here in Cambridge by meanes of this 2^d Visitation (wch is very sharp) y^t we must of necessity begg. J haue to this purpose made bold to inclose a letter to my L^d of London, not knowing how to direct it in case he should be at Fulham, but desiring it may be speedily wth. him, which J doubt not to be effect[ed] by y^r meanes. J know you will be ready to promote soe charitable a worke,

S^{r.}

Y^r most affectionate Servt

FRA: WILSON

To the Reverend & his hon^red friend
  Dr Sancroft Dean of St Pauls
London
near St Pauls

In his absence to be conveyed to
  the Right Reverend father in
    g^d the B^p of London.

Bishop Henchman to Dean Sancroft.

Mr. Deane   [Undated]
His Matie. hath declared his pleasure that a solemn Humiliation shall be observed throughout the Kingdome: and hath commaunded my Lord of Canterburie that a Litourgie be forthwith prepared for that vse: whereupon his Grace requires you and me to consider of a Forme: which may soone be done for there hath been frequent occasions of that kind of Service: and there is no further labour for vs but to frame some Collects, all other parts may be vsed with little or no alterations. Jf you haue ready at hand any former Services be pleased to bring them with you here you shall find that of 1625. 1636. and 1640. Jf you can be here to morrow before dinner we shall finish the work before you goe away. The Lord preserve you.

Your very affectionate

Fulham: prsh.   Brother
    S^{ti.} Petri   HUMFR: LONDON

For Reuerend Dr. Sancroft
Deane of St. Pauls in Angell
Court neare St. Gregories Church.

[140]

Stephen Bing to Dean Sancroft.
[London], 24 July, 1665.

Reverend S^{r.}

 . . . .

Mr. Iuett, Price Fisher Warner are out of Town & m^{r.} Webb allmost, for he is not so often wth us as I wish he were. Mr. Sub Deane, Masters Clifford & Quaterman whoe only speake of going out of Towne are dilligent & all so 3 of the Vicars Mr. Cockrey, Simpson, & Morrice th'others are out of the City. I intend God willing to keep close to his Wor^{p.} in the Church except great hazard should befall mee. Dr. Barwick . . . resolues his continuance here, for any thing he knowes. The Lord in mercy look upon us: its said there willbe a great increase this week of the last bill wch was 1089. its more in St. Gregories then at your departure. & in an Alley in Pater Noster Rowe & a man & his wife fallen sick in the Petti Canons what the issue of it will be Thursday next will more informe yo^{u.} . . . Wee haue the Prayer & Service performed [3 times a day] as you ordered & that in time & with a reverentiall decency & a comely congregacon considering the times frequenting those solemnities. . . .

  Hon^{ed} Sr. Your most Faithfull Servant.
    STEPHEN BING.

Same to same.
27th July, 1665

S^r

 . . . .

People frequent ye Church as before excepting on Sundays and ye last Holyday on wch wee had a Sermon & shall haue another on the Fast Day: The increase of Gods Judgm^t: deads peoples hearts that trading strangely ceaseth & bills of Exchange are not accepted so y^t they shutt up their shopps & such a feare possesseth them as its wonderfull to see how they hurry into the Country as though ye same God were not there y^t is in ye City so that those that are living and liued in ye great sickness time saw, nor knew not yᵉ like when there dyed 4000 a week. I pray God to pʳvent a sad Sequel. Great complaint there is of necessity & needs must it be yᵉ more when yᵉ rich hast away yᵗ should supply yᵉ pores want. I haue been since the writing of my last lr: in sevrall places, being informed of some yᵗ were shut up to be in a very necessitous condicon to see if it were so or no, & so finding them I haue been bold to extend yoʳ charity to yᵉ outrunning yᵉ bank you honᵉᵈ me with. . . .

> Your Worᵖˢ most humble
> & faithfull Servant
> STEPHEN BING

Dr. Peter Barwick to Dean Sancroft.

Lond. Aug. 3, 1665.

Mʳ· Dean

. . . .

Wee haue noe neighbours left in yᵉ court [off Ave Marie Lane] besides a Goldsmith of my own trade, but Mʳ· Fleetham locks up yᵉ Avennues every night. We haue several houses infected in the Parish, and one of yoʳ· own out of wᶜʰ· Mʳˢ· gallson and one other are dead but God be thanked there is noe fresh house infected within yᵉ· Parish these 10 days that I know of. . . .

> Sʳ· yoʳ· humble servant
> PE: BARWICK

These
To yᵉ Reverend Dʳ· William
Sancroft Dean of Sᵗ· Pauls
at yᵉ Rose and Crown
    at TUNBRIDGE
        Post pd

Rev· Stephen Bing to Dean Sancroft.

3 August 1665.

Reverend & right Worˡˡ·

There are now but 3 Petti Canons left vizt. my
selfe Mr. Clifford & Masters wth 2 Vicars Mr. Simpson &
Morrice, the rest are out of Towne: Mr. Portington lies
at the poinct of death whose turne being to officiat this
week J supply for none els would doe it except they were
payd for it: Little mercy the Lord be mercifull to us; J
wish it were as formerly wch was not so in such case of
necessity. . . .

Your Wor^{ps.} most humble & affectionate Servt.
STEPHEN BINGE

Its s^{d.} that my L. B^{p.} of London hath sent to those Pastors
that haue quitted their flocks by reason of these times y^{t.}
if they returne not speedily others will be put into their
places.

Dr. Barwick to Dean Sancroft.

Lond. Aug. 5, 1665.

Mr. Dean

Give me leaue to discharge the part of a frend and to
tell you what J haue thought perhaps of noe great moment.
Jt will be noe news to tell you (for you will easily imagin
it) that ye mouths of a slanderous generation are wide
enough open against those that are with drawn both of yor.
profession and ours; but one of my neighbours told me
(who J indeed think wishes well both to you and to y^e
Church) that it was wondered that you would goe, and not
leaue any thing that they had heard of behind you for y^e
poor neighbours. J tould him that in what Cases it was
lawfull to goe was not in the skill of every one to deter-
mine; but as for yor. goeing to ye Wells you had resolved it,
and by my advice, long before any plague was heard of, and
as for yor. charity to ye poor J knew you had given a Considerable summe (to a Parish that a little money would
not releeve) before you went. . . .

Stephen Bing to Dean Sancroft.

7th. August: 1665

Reverend & right Wor^{ll}:

God hath been pleased now to encompas us wth his pestelentiall hand, in 3 places in Carter Lane, in Sermon Lane wch. is next my house, in ye Lane at ye end of Knightriders street wch. Leadeth up to yor Co^{rt.,} in Ave Mary Lane in the Buildings where ye B^{p.} of London: howse was & in an Alley in Paternoster row & on the backside in ye Shambles wth severall besides in Christ Church parish in St. Bennets Pauls Wharfe where its said died 3 ye last night & 5 was buryed then out of St. Gregories & others died; its s^{d.} likewise to be in St. Andrews in ye Wardrop: yet nevertheles under ye shadow of ye Almighty shall be my refuge until this calamity be overpast. . . .

Your most humble & affectionat Servt.

STEPHEN BING

These
To ye Reverend & right Wor^{ll.}
Willm. Sancroft Doctor of Divinity,
Deane of ye Cathedrall Church of
St. Paul London.
        Present.
To be left at y^e
Rose & Crowne in
Tunbridge.

Same to same.

10 August 1665.

Reverend & right Wor^{ll.}

I haue sent yo^u ye Thursdays Intelligence, half of wch was in th'other sent on Munday wch. I hope is receaued . . .; likewise ye weekly Bill wch. is very sad; and ye more sad are our times y^t neither calme nor storme will abate ye fury of monstrous spirits whoe in ye face of a Congregacon as at Pauls th'other day, will say these calamities are caused by ye Government in Church & State. The sicknes is break out in 2 places more since Munday in St. Gregories one dwelling opening into yor yard & th'other at ye left corner of ye Entry of our going into

yᵉ Church; Its in Cambridg also of wᶜʰ I forgot to tell
youᵘ. and whereas I told of 2 sick in yᵉ Petti Canons, Its
sᵈ. the Husband died of a Consumpcon but yᵉ wife lies
sick of a pl: so as for other places infected in yᵉ Parish
I informed in my last. . . .

Your most humble & faithfull Servᵗ.

STE. BING

Dʳ. Barwick yᵉ constant frequenter of our Church sometimes 3 times in a day remembers his service to yoʳ. worᵖ.

J. Tillison to Dean Sancroft.

London August yᵉ 10ᵗʰ. 1665

Reuend Sʳ

.   .   .   .

J have not heard from Dʳ Pory since he left London
nor do I know how to send to him though his mayd once
took a resolution to abide by it; yet it seemes she is fled.
. . . I doubt yoʳ wood will hardly be brought to London
this somer for I doubt it impossible to gett a Boat to fetch
it; yet I haue made it my businesse 2 days together to hire
Lighters & can not gett any except one yᵗ will not fetch it
vnder 2ˢ yᵉ Load heretofore yᵉ Church gaue but 14ᵈ yᵉ
Load. . . .

Reuend Sʳ

Yoʳ faithfull humble Sʳᵗ

JO: TILLISON

Same to same.

August yᵉ 15ᵗʰ: 1665

Reverend Sʳ

.   .   .   .

J hope yᵘ will not take my simple well meaning amiss
nor take it ill if J put yᵘ in minde of our own Pish where
there is all this tyme 16 or 17 houses vissitted, a great
many of them poore & in want, & yᵗ some of yᵉ Pishonʳˢ
as J am informed (j beg yoʳ Pdon for my good will) doe
alittle grumble yᵗ youᵘ left nothing for yᵉ poore when yᵘ

[145]

went away. I Pceive since this, that m^r Bing had ye disposing of some of yor charity & J do not doubt but y^t he will give y^u an account of it. nor do J think it is yor will y^t any Ptiallity should be vsed in this case. it is very Pobable y^t some neighbouring Pishes may stand in need, but J am sure y^t ye miserable condicon of St Giles'es Criplegate which is one of yor peculiars, is more to be pittied then any Pish in or about London where all have liberty least the sick & poore should be famished within dores the Pish not being able to relieue their necessities. J had, not long since such a su[me] as yo^{rs} to distribute, & where J knew not ye necessity of ye poore J pd a su[me] to ye Churchwardens & they to ye overseers of ye poore soe y^t J had an account brought to how many Psons in each Pish it was distributed. but this is no rule for yo^u: Yo^r neighbour & Tenn^t ffleetham has his health god be thanked very well, & though his mayd was reported to be dead with his child she is recoued & all ye family well. Dr Barwick is very carefull of him & his family & of keeping ye gates duly lockt vp. I was lately att ffullham & my L^d [Bishop of London] comanded me to let y^u know y^t himselfe & family are all in good health. . . . J am not certain whether J shall remoue from this place or no. . . . J smoke yor house twice a week, Tuesdayes & frydayes. . . .

Yo^r obedient humble S^{rt}

J. TILLISON

Same to same

London August ye 23th 1665

Reverend S^r

Yo^{rs} of Satterday last from Ewell, J have recd. And as far as in me lyes have observed & done yor comands. J have payd 40^{li} to Mr Daniell Keilway [Kelloway?], & 5^{li} to those of ye Choire to whom yo^u directed mee, who returne theire humble service & thankes, & promise to continue theire constant attendance in ye service of ye Church. J likewise payd 5^{li} to ye Churchwardens of St Gyles's Criplegate since yor last to me, ye rest of yor charity J hope m^r Bing will give a good account of it. he had 5^{li}

of yor last mony from me. Though yor care could not have been more than it was for furnishinge me with mony to discharge those paym^{ts.} wch yo^u ordered in yor last, yet all those wayes failed every one. Dr Barwick pretended yesterday y^t he had not soe much mony of his owne to disburse p^rsently, but att ye last (though alittle scrupled at first) he was willing to let me take 40^{li} out of ye Comonstock & y^t we intended to doe this morninge, but god almighty has ordred it otherwise, by strikeinge Dr Barwick with so desperate sicknesse y^t it was not fitt for me to goe to him, nor he in Condicon to be reminded of any such thinge. it seemes not one member but all the parts of his body beares a Parte in his sufferinges, neither riseinge nor botch^e does yet appeare. a slow weake Pulse & faintnesse possesses him, his sweating is not much. Seeing this to happen it made me void of hope to effect my businesse, yea & danted me very much too. But after a little Pause J went to Sr Robt Viners (there m^r welsted's mony lyes) but could not receive one penny vnlesse J brought m^r welsted's note. J am sorry m^r welsted should forget his promise. he is some where towards Vxbridge.

Yo^r Tenn^t ffleetham dyed this afternoon. Kendrick ye Bellringer has languished since last Sonday we have some hopes this eveninge y^t he may recover. Johnson yor Bayliff was buried last night. . . .

Yo^r faithfull S^{vt}
JO: TILLISON.

Same to same.

Sept: 14th. 1665.

Reuend S^r

. . . .

Dr Barwick is past all appearances of danger god be praised. . . . The Sacrist is not att home & his wife is dead by ye comon disease. . . . Wee are in good hopes y^t god in his mercy will putt a stop to this sad calamity of sicknesse. But ye desolacon of ye Citty is very great, y^t heart is either steel or stone y^t will not lament for this sad visitation, & will not bleed for those vnutterable sorrowes. it is a tyme god knowes y^t one Woe courts another, those y^t are sick are in extream sorrow, ye poore are in need those y^t are in health are in feare of infecon on ye one side, & ye wicked intentions of hellish rebellious spiritts to put vs in an vproar on ye other side. what ey: would not weep to see soe many habitacons vninhabited? ye poore sick not vissited? ye hungry not fed? ye grave not satisfyed? Death stares vs continually in ye face in every infected Person y^t passeth by vs, in every coffin wch is dayly & hourely carried along ye streets: ye Bells never cease to putt vs in minde of our mortallity. The custom was in ye beginninge to bury ye Dead in ye night onely, now both night and day will hardly be tyme enough to do it, for ye last weeks mortality did too apparently evidence that, that ye Dead was piled in heapes above ground for some houres together before either tyme could be gained or place to bury them in. The Quakers (as we are informed) have buryed in theire peece of ground 1000 for some weekes together last past. many are dead in Ludgate, Newgate & X^t church hospitall & many other places about ye towne wch are not included in ye bill of Mortality. The disease it self (as is acknowledged by our Praction^{rs} in Physick) was more favourable in ye beginninge of ye contagion: now more feirce & violent — and they themselves do like wise confesse to stand amazed to meet with soe many various Symptomes wch they finde amongst theire patients. one week y^e gen^{rll} distempers are botches & Biles; y^e next week as cleare skind as may be, but death spares neither, one week full of spotts & tokens; & Phaps y^e succeeding bill none at all. Now taken with a vomitting & loosnesse & within 2 or 3 dayes almost a gen$^{rll.}$ rageing madnesse. one while Patients vse to linger 4 or 5 dayes att other tymes not 48 houres. & att this very tyme we finde it more quick then ever it was. many are sick: and few escape. where it has had its fling there it decreases where it has not been long, there it increases. it raigned most heretofore in Alleys &c: now it domineers in ye open streets. Y^e poorer sort was most afflicted, now yᵉ richer beare a share. Capᵗ Colchester is dead. ffleetham & all his family are clearly swept away except one mayd. Dʳ Burnett Dʳ Glover & one or 2 more of yᵉ Colledge of Physitians wᵗʰ Dʳ O Dowd wᶜʰ was licensed by my Lᵈˢ Grace of Canterbury, some surgeons, Apothecaryes, & Johnson yᵉ Chymist dyed all very suddenly. some say (but god forbid yᵗ J should report it for truth) that these in a consultacon together, if not all yet yᵉ greatest parte of them attempted to open a dead corpse wᶜʰ was full of yᵉ tokens & being in hand with yᵉ dissected body some fell down dead imediately & others did not out live yᵉ next day att Noone. All is well & in safety att yoʳ house god be thanked.

Brimstone, hops, Peppr & ffrankincense Sr: j vse to fume ye roomes with— Vpon Tuesday last J made it my dayes work to kindle fires in every roome of yᵉ house where J could do it. & aired all yᵉ bed clothes & bedding att yᵉ fires & soe let them all lye ly abroad vntil this morning yᵉ feather bed in yᵉ back chamber was almost spoiled with yᵉ heavy weight of Carpetts & other things vpon it.— J ame afrayd I have been too tedious & therefore beg yoʳ Pdon & take my leave who am

(Reuend Sʳ)

Yoʳ most faithfull humble serᵗ

JO: TILLISON.

Same to same.

Reuend Sʳ   October yᵉ 12ᵗʰ: 1665

.   .   .   .

J am afrayd yᵘ will have a very slender account of yoʳ Tennᵗˢ this Quarter. ffleetham, swinston & his wife, Gulstone & his wife, & halfe a dozen masters of familyes are dead: wᵗʰ many more in other familyes. . . .

Yoʳ most obedient faithfull serᵗ

JO: TILLISON

John Overing to Dean Sancroft.

London 2ᵈ: Nov. 1665.

Right Worpˡˡ

In right humble manner I presume to acquaint you, that yᵉ Rectory of Sᵗ Mary Maudlins Old fishstreete in

[149]

London in your Worps guift is now void by the death of the late reverend divine D^r: Matthew Griffith. J know that in duetie J am bound to waite on you in person, to giue you an account hereof, but by reason of the dainger of the times, and the unkindnesse of country people to Londoners, J cannot performe it; not knowing whether at this time it might be accepted by your worp. And therefore in hopes of your worps pardon, J have writ these lines, humbly desiring your gracious acceptance of them. . . . J am incouraged to present this, my humble Supplication, earnestly desiring that your worp will vouch safe to conferr the said Rectory upon your humble petitioner. J haue (Right Worp^{ll}) supplyed the cure during all these times of sicknesse, and mortality; and shall yet (God assisting) wth: your worps leaue take the same care of it upon me: hoping that your worp at your returne to London will grant this request of your humble Supplicant. J shall not further trouble your worp at present, but Subscribe my selfe*

The meanest of yor worps serv^{ts}:

JOHN OUERING.

George Davenport to Dean Sancroft.

Durham Castle Dec 4 1665

Mr Dean;

. . . . In the first place, God be praised, we are all well. And I do not hear that any place either in the County or Diocesse is infected with the pestilence. . . .

From a

Petition of the Rev. Anselm Herford for the Rectory of St. Mary Magdalene, Old Fish St.

London, Decemb ye 9th 1665.

Most Reuerend S^r

.   .   .   .

Blessed be ye God of heauen it hath pleased his mercie

---

*This is a sample of numerous applications made toward the close of 1665 for vacancies in the Church as a result of the Plague. One of these was written on a half sheet of paper as ''less prejudiciall fro an infected city.''

—Harl. MSS. No. 3785, fol. 41.

to preserue me Wonderfullie. When soe manie yea and soe manie ministers too are swept away. I lodged Jn your Worships rents [*i. e.* with the tenants] because I would be neere the praiers of St Pauls & of y^t familie J lodged with ther's not a soule aliue but it pleas'd god to giue me warning before he graciouslie struck the fatall blow. . . .

John Cosin, Bishop of Durham to Dean Sancroft.
Durham Castle Jan^ry 22. 1665[-6].
Mr Deane of St Pauls.

.   .   .   .

The Sicknes in these parts thankes be to God is well abated though it lurketh still in some of our Quarter, for ye maintenance of those that have been and still are infected, wee have been put to lay a Sesse upon the Countrey so small were ye Contribucons of the severall Parishes throughout all my Diocess, but J have now good hope that upon the Account made me both of those Contribucons and Assessm^ts: J shall be able to spare 50^li to be sent unto my Lord [Bishop] of London towards the help of those that are infected still in this City. J shall have ye Amount given me on thrsday and if J find so much money remaining J will return it to his Lordship by a Bill of Exchange to Sr Wm Turner by ye morrowes post, so wishing you all good health and hapines J rest

S^r
Yo^r very affectionate ffriend
JO: D

George Davenport to Dean Sancroft.
Durham Castle. Jan. 23. 1665[-6].
Sir; the business of this is to convey the enclosed, wch tells of money sent for ye poor of London, though the plague is again at Gatside, & this County hath been taxed about 250^l for y^t place & others y^t have been infected. . . .

y^r humble Servant,
G. D.

Joseph Beaumont to Dean Sancroft.

S[r]

. . . .

I purpos this day to acquaint our Vicechancell[r] with what you write touching y[e] D. of Xtchurch his charity to poor Cambr. Last week none dyed of y[e] Plague in y[e] Town; onely One at y[e] Pest House, but this week it has fallen into a new house in S. Clements parish, & one Woman dead of it.

S. Peters Coll   JSPH BEAUMONT.
Febr. 1. 1665[-6]

APPENDIX I

FROM THE *Autobiography,* AND UNPUBLISHED LETTERS
OF THE REV. SYMON PATRICK, RECTOR OF
ST. PAUL'S, COVENT GARDEN.

At the end of 1664 was a very hard frost, which lasted
from Christmas till near the middle of April in the year
1665, when the plague began to break out, a little after the
breaking of the frost. The next month, May 13th, I went to
drink Astrop waters; where I stayed a month, and there
met that great man Dr. Willis; who understanding that I
intended to return to London, and look after my parish,
was wonderfully kind to me, and directed me how to order
myself, and often in the time of the plague wrote to me
and sent me money to give to the poor.

After a short visit which I paid to my father and
mother, I returned to London in July, where I found the
plague already broke out in my parish, notwithstanding
which, I resolved to commit myself to the care of God in
the discharge of my duty, and accordingly preached July
23rd. when I had many heavenly meditations in my mind,
and found the pleasure wherewith they filled the soul was far
beyond all the pleasure of the flesh. Nor could I fancy any
thing would last so long, nor give me such joy and delight,
as those thoughts which I had of the other world, and the
taste which God vouchsafed me of it. . . . About the middle
of August I set myself to write a short exhortation to those
who were shut up because of the plague, and just when I
had finished it heard the melancholy news of my father's
death, on the 15th; upon which I wrote a letter to comfort
my mother, wherewith I much comforted myself; . . . And
on the 30th. I thought of writing a little treatise of comfort in this sad time, which I finished and sent to my
bookseller September the first, praying the blessing of

Heaven might attend upon these my little labours for the good of souls.

On the 3rd my brother was taken very ill, and vomited forty or fifty times, and my servant also had a swelled face, and I myself also had a sore pain in my leg, which broke my sleep, and made me suspect some touch of the plague, which was now come to its height, there dying ten thousand in one week. But blessed be God all these maladies went over without danger. On the 9th I set myself to consider the great goodness of God to me since this plague, and how many dangers I had been in by people coming to speak to me out of infected houses, and by my going to those houses to give them money, which was sent to me by charitable persons to distribute to them in need. Particularly Sir William Jones sent me fifty pounds, and many other things which I have noted in a little book, but shall now [not?] here rehearse. One thing I cannot but remember, that preaching a funeral sermon at Battersea, I was desired to let a gentleman come back to London in a coach which I had hired to wait upon me. The gentleman proved an apothecary, who entertained me all the way home with a relation of all the many people he had visited, who had the plague, how they were affected, with the nature of their swellings and sores. But blessed be God, I was not in the least affrighted, but let him go on, without any conceit that he might infect me.

My poor clerk, a very honest man, found his house infected, and acquainted me with it. I was so pitiful as to bid him come out of the house himself, and attend his business, and I should not be afraid of him. He did so, and his wife and child died of the plague; but he was preserved, and had a thankful remembrance of my kindness to his dying day, many years after.

On the 15th of October I preached a sermon, (when the plague began to abate very much) of the remembrance we ought to have of the time of affliction, when God restores to prosperity. It was upon consideration of Psalm xxxviii, whose title is 'a Psalm to bring to remembrance;' wherein

I wished them to set down in writing all that they found observable in the late time of danger; their thoughts, their promises and vows, their good resolutions, &c., and to write at the head of them, 'A meditation to bring to remembrance.' And accordingly I noted how good God had been to myself, not only in preserving my life, but giving so much health, and enabling me with cheerfulness to go through my labours; resolving to do my duty still more faithfully for the time to come.

—FROM THE *Autobiography of Symon Patrick*, PP. 51-56.

FROM THE UNPUBLISHED CORRESPONDENCE BETWEEN SYMON PATRICK AND ELIZABETH GAUDEN.*

Add. Mss. 5,810.

Covent Gard Wednesd Morn:

Aug: 8. 1665.

. . . . . .

If you think there is any Danger from these Papers, which you receive, the Fire, I suppose, will expell it, if you let them see it before they come to your Hands. . . .

For Mrs. Gauden   S. P.

 at Hutton-Hall in Essex, these.

Same to same.

Sat: Sept: 8. 1665.

. . . . . .

It was a lovely Season yesterday, & we hoped for some sweete cleare Weather: but it please God, the Wind is changed againe, & brings Abundance of Raine with it: & indeed we have no settled Weather since I saw you, which hath made the Sicknesse, I believe, rage more: for *South Winds* are alwayes observed to be *bad* in such *Times*: & the Wind stays not long out of that Quarter. It decreases in some Places, & grows very much in others. I hope there will not so many dye here [in St. Pauls, C. G.] as did last week; & yet we have 21 or 22 dead already. I suppose you think I

---

* I am not certain whether this Mrs. Gauden was wife of Dr. J. Gauden (then minister at Bocking in Essex, and afterwards Archbishop of Canterbury), or Sir Denis Gauden of the Victualling Office. There are two conflicting opinions on the first leaf of the MS. volume containing these letters.

intend to stay here still; though I understand by your Question you would not have mee. But, my Friend, what am I better than another? Somebody must stay here: and is it fit I should set such a value upon myself, as my going away, & leaving another will signify? For it will, in effect be to say, That I am too good to be lost, but is no matter if another bee. Truly I do not think myself so considerable to the World: & though my Friends set a great Price upon mee, yet that Temptation hath not yet made me of that Mind: and I know their Love makes me pass for more with them then I am worth. When I mention that Word, Love, I confesse, it moves me much, & I have a great Passion for them, & wish I might live to embrace them once again: but I must not take any undue Courses to satisfye this Passion, which is but too strong in mee. I must let Reason prevaille, & stay with my Charge, which I take hitherto to be my Duty, whatever come. I cannot tell what Good wee do their Soules, though I preach to those who are well, and write to those who are ill, (I mean print little Papers for them, which yet are too big to send by the Post;) but I am sure, while I stay here, I shall do Good to their Bodies, & perhaps save some from perishing; which I look upon as a considerable End of my continuing. My dear Friend, do not take it ill, that I cannot comply with your Desire on this Thing; you see what sways mee, & I know that you will yield to it, & that it ought to be stronger then the Love of you. If you can convince mee, that I may, with a good Conscience, go, you may think it will be acceptable: but I know not upon what Grounds you will make it good. Try, if you have a mind. But if I should go, why would you have me be at *Clapham,* when my *Brother* is so neare, & you are not there? . . . Perhaps you meane, that I should be there on Week Dayes, and preach here on Lords Dayes. But that will be dangerous perhaps both to them & to mee: at least to them: & I have not hitherto layne out one Night since you left *Clapham.* . . . May I not buy a Paire of Stockins, of a Friend, whom I can be confident is not infected, & which have layne long in his Shop? I want nothing else at present. And how should it be more dangerous then to receive Bear & Wine, the Vessells being capable of Infection? but especially Bread, they say, is the most attractive of it, which I am forced to buy: for I know not otherwayes to have it. I saw last Tuesday about 30 People in the Strand, with white Sticks in their Hands, & the D^r of the Pest House walking in his gowne before them. The first Woman rid on a Horse, & had a Paper Flag on top of her Stick, with Laus Deo written on it. They were going to the Iustices, being poore People sent thither, & recovered by him of the Plague. He seemed to take no small Content in his stately March before them. But now I have told Tales of myself, & confessed that I go sometimes Abroad. Indeed, it cannot be well helpt, & I hope there is no great Danger. I will not grow bold, & confident by being safe so long, nor would I grow timorous, as such Case as you require, I doubt, will make mee. I saw a Letter from *Salisbury* of the 6 Instant, which saith, now the Plague has broke out there, & his *Majesty* will be gone suddenly. He hath *not been well of late,* and imagines that Aire doth not agree with him. This is true: for it comes from one of my Parish there, who is well acquainted att the Court. Now I must make and End, & only add my hearty Love to all with you, & your Friends, praying for your Preservation, & remaining y^rs most affectionately

S. P.

I forgot to tell you, that instead of the *Plague Drink* you writ of, they have sent me *Plague Water,* or some such Thing; for it is *distilled* & nothing like what I had before: but never trouble them to send me any. *Dr Michael Thwayle* directed to make, & drink presently of *London Treacle* & *Lady Allen's Water.* I bought both presently, but forgot to mix them. Only now and then I take a little Treacle.

For my Honoured Friend
Mrs Gauden att Hutton-Hall.
Leave this at the White Hart in Burntwood, Essex.

Same to same.

Sat: Night. Sept: 30. 1665.

My Friend.

    .   .   .   .   .   .

    You enquire *what Ministers are dead?* for you heard of
some & would know the Truth. There are more, to tell you
plainly, then the Number you name. *M*ʳ· *Peachall*, & *M*ʳ·
Mandrill, who were *lecturers*, dyed a good while ago: *one*
of them *Lecturer of S*ᵗ· *Clement's*, the *other* at *Benet Fink.*
Since, there dyed one *M*ʳ· *Austin, minister,* I think, of *S*ᵗ·
Mary Stainings: the *minister of Alphage,* whose Name, I
think, was *M*ʳ· *Stone.* One *M*ʳ· *Bastwick,* (son to the *famous Doctor of that Name*) who was *Preacher at the
Counter in the Poultrye; M*ʳ· *Welbank,* one of the ministers
of *S*ᵗ· *Saviour's, Southwark*: *M*ʳ· *Throchmorton, Curate of
S*ᵗ· *George's, Southwark*: & a *Gentleman* who *officiated* for
*M*ʳ· *Hall* in *Bastshaw.* All these I can call to mind; and the
mention of *this last,* whos *Name,* I think, was *Phillips,*
brings a *sad story* to my mind, which I will relate, because
something depends upon it which I ought to remember. On
Tuesday was Fortnight, I was at Dʳ· Owtram's, & *M*ʳ· *Bastwick,* whom I spake of, came in, whom *I never saw before,*
and the Doctor *not often.* He came to make a *Visit,* but the
*D*ʳ· has no *Acquaintance* with him, only had met him at a
Friend's. He had all the Newes of the Towne, & particularly told us of the death of *that Gentleman* who supplied
*M*ʳ· *Hall's* Place. He was left in Trust to pay him his Money
every *Munday*; & he told us how timourous he was, & carefull, that he would scarce come into his House to receive it:
& that he preached the Sunday sennight before, but was
dead, with his wife, & all his Children (which were 3) before
Thursday Night. The next Time I met *D*ʳ· *Outram,* he told
mee, that *M*ʳ· *Bastwick* went from us Home, & fell sick that
very night, & dyed a few Days after, I think on *Sunday.*
The *D*ʳ· added, that he did not like his looks then, & thought
there was a great Alteration in his Countenance; but he said
nothing to me when he was gone, (which was about 5
o'Clock) though to his Man he gave a Charge (as he tells

me) that if he came againe, he should not let him in, but say,
he could not be spoken withall. You see how much wee are
beholden to God in keeping us from the Dangers to which
we are exposed. M^r. Lance in Lombard Street also is dead
lately, but not of the Sicknesse. The *minister of Kentish
Town* hath had it, & is recovered. I think I have heard of
another or *two,* that were *Curates* but of *no more Ministers,*
The last Weeke gave us great Encouragement to hope for
the Restoration of better Health: but I am something afraid
this Week will raise it againe alittle: for wee have 15 or 16
dead already, and had but *19 last Weeke in all.* It is fit
perhaps that it should be so, least men impute all to the
cold weather, & nothing to *God's Goodnesse.* The more in-
scrutable this Disease is, & beyond the Account of Men,
the more are they directed to acknowledge a supreme Power
that chastises men, & corrects their Disobedience. There
are People who rely upon *pitifull* Things, as *containe
Tokens* of its goeing away shortly. I have been told, more
then once, of the *falling out of the Clapper of the great Bell
at Westminster,* which they say, it did before the last Great
Plague ended: & this they take for a very *comfortable Sign.
Others* speake of the *Dawes* more frequenting the *Pallace
& Abbey,* which, if true, is a better Sign, supposing the Aire
to have been *infected.* For the Bookes I read tell mee, that
the goeinge away of Birds is the *Forerunner* of the *Plague,*
& that one shall *see few* in a *Plague Yeare.* The *Death of
Birds* in *Houses* when they are *caged, ordinarily preceedes*
the *Death* of the *Inhabitants*: for these aiery *Creatures* feale
the *Alteration* in that *Element sooner* then *wee.* Thus you
see how desirous all are *for some Token for Good* & how
they catch at the smallest Shadowes for it. But the *best
Sign* of all, I doubt, is much wanting: & that is, the *Refor-
mation of mens manners,*—of which I heare little; unlesse
that those come to Church, who did not before. . . . A sad
Thing, that the Event of these Iudgments proves no better!
But so it comonly falls out, & men soon forget both their
Smart, & also the good Resolutions which it formed. I
hope, my Friend, the Hand of God will not be without its

a great Wisdome, as well as Iustice, in this Restraint which I now suffer, & therefore I thankfully accept it, & intreat you to assist mee with your Prayers, that I may both understand the meaning of it, & likewise make the right use which God intends. I must ever also acknowledge a wonderfull Kindnesse of God to mee mixed with this; for I am well & chearfull to my Admiration & Astonishment, when I seriously think of it. I could not have expected to spend my Time, & find it so little a Burden to mee, as it used now & then to be when I was alone. The long Evenings, when I see none (I give God Thanks) pass away without any Irksomenesse at all. I have quite changed my Diet. I eat boiled Meats & Broth more then I used: something at Supper also, which does not hinder my Thoughts. You see I take Care of myself, & by this long Letter will perceive that you are much in the Thoughts of your ever affect: Friend

S. P.

Sat: Night, Oct: 7. 1665.

I have taken a little *Cold,* which hath put some Damp upon my Spirits—I knew it would be so,—for I felt the Wind strike into my Head as I was burying a Corpse one Night. That is a Thing I have oft found prejudiciall: but *there is no Body else to do it now.* I think too sometimes I have too great a Burden of Worke upon mee: but hitherto I go through it very well; only I am sometimes a little weary after *preaching twice;* especially when the *Fast Week* comes. It comes now & then into my *Wishes,* that I was more free from this Kind of Buisinesse in a Parish; for I suppose I could profitably employ my Time in some other Way. But I check myself in this & a great many other Wishes, knowing there is *no Contentment* but in *conforming* our Wills to our *present Conditions.* . . . [1] Wee are in great Hopes of a considerable *Decrease* this Week. *Here* indeed wee have *buried* many, & *so they do at Westminster,* as Dr. *Outram* tells mee; but in *other Places* the *Bells do not go so*

---

[1] After the Plague, Patrick was raised to the bishopric of Chichester and, later, to that of Ely.

Instruction to us, & that wee shall be carefull, if he let us live, to improve it as we ought. I cannot but acknowledge *oft*. I must correct an *Error* in my last but one Mr. *Welbank* is *not dead*, as was reported: it is the *Curate*, one Mr. *Knightley*, who, they say, did not dye of the Sicknesse neither. This was *Occasion* of the *Report* that Mr. *Shillingfleet* was *dead; the Reader of St. Andrew's Holborne dying* a good while ago; but as for Mr. *Shillingfleet* he has *not beene here along Time* but gets his Place supplyed by somebody. . . .

> Yours very affectionately,
>
> *S. P.*

Octob: 12. [1665].

My Friend,

It happens to be such a bright Night, that I cannot say all that I would. I have not had so many Burialls a great while, & I deferred to write till Night, being with my *Brother* at *Battersea* all Day. The *Sicknesse* is *not decreased* so much as wee expected: but wee ought to be very thankful for any Abatement. There are *652 less* this Week then the last. There *dyed here* [in my Parish] but *15*, which is *10* less then the *Weeke before*. How it will be this Week I know not; but there are *9 dead already, 6 being buried to Night*. In the next *Parish of St. Martin's* there dyed *no more to Day*, which gives Hope still of a Decrease there. The Sicknesse is much at *Wandsworth*, where *24 dyed* in one *Week*. It is got into *Wiltshire* also, & is very neare *Sir W. St. Iohn's*, so that they have sent their Children away to Mr. *Bernard's* neare *Huntingdon*. It is a very sad Time I perceive every where, & I must acknowledge it a very singular Favour of God, that I am so much supported. I hope I shall not forget his Goodnesse if he let me live to see more healthfull & pleasant Seasons. He knows how long it is necessary to keep us under, & how much Time is Requisite to make us thoroughly serious. If that be but effected, we shall have a more sober Ioy hereafter. . . .

> *S. P.*

Covent Garden, Oct. 14 [1665]

. . . .

People are grown bold, & because they find themselves well, they think their Neighbours ought not to shun them, though they have some dye of the Plague in their Houses. In many Places they do not shut them up, & so they take their Liberty to come abroad; and there also when they need not, & where they ought to be more civill. But wee must not expect that from ordinary People: it is a Thing proper to better bred Souls. If the Vulgar be not intollerably rude, we are beholden to them.

From your affectionate Friend

S^y. *Patrick*.

Octob: 17. [1665].

. . . .

Wee expect a very great *abatement* this *Week* in the *Whole,* though here [in my Parish] wee buried *one more* then *last Week.* The *Citty Remembrancer* told a Friend of mine, that there are *1500 lesse without the Walls* then *last Week,* beside the *Decrease* in the *Citty.* I heare M^r. *Iohn Goodwin* is *dead* somewhere in Essex. It is said that D^r. *Bolton* also is *dead* in the *Country* whether *he went* because of the Contagion.

I am your affect: Friend

S. P.

Oct: 21. [1665].

. . . .

M^r. *Cradock* writes me word, he hath a great mind *to return,* tho' there is *no Term here,* & I think he will have no *Employment.* . . .

My poor Clarke . . . hath had *his Family sadly visited.* His *Wife & 7 Children* (all he hath) have beene all sicke: & now his *Wife & one Child* are *dead, & she big with Child.* The Rest are like to *do well,* & I hope I have saved the poor Man by timely Advice to remove himself, that he may take Care of all the Rest.

Your affectionate Friend,

S. P.

Nov: 7. 1665.

My Friend,

I have made further Enquiries about the Accesse of People to London, & their State of Health since they came, but can find no Ground for those sad Reports which you have. This I find, that the same Storyes are spread in other Countries, & People are thereby affrighted from coming thither: but there is no Cause, as farre as I can learne. Yesterday I met M^r. Holliard, (who askt very kindly of you) who told mee he heard 2 Linen Drapers in Cornwall were returned, & dead: but he enquired of their Neighbours, & they knew of no such Thing. Yet I think my Church-Warden says well, That of all the Lyes he hath heard, he thinks this will do least Harm: for it will keep People from flocking too fast to London, which otherwise they might be apt to do. The Soldiers (who have hitherto beene quartered in Tents in Hyde Park) returned yesterday into the Citty; I suppose because of the Weather, which may indanger their Healths more then this Place. . . .

[S. P.]

Nov: 9. [1665].

My deare Friend.

I suppose you will heare before this can reach you, that the Sicknesse did not decrease so much last Week, but it has increased as much in this that is nearly past—I have walked to Battersea and back againe with a great Deale of Ease this Day. They have had none dye there this Fort-night; but at Wandsworth there is still a great Mortality: there are 12 dead since Sunday, as one of the Parish tells mee. You may think the Increase of the Sicknesse here comes from the Accesse of more People: but I think it is otherwise: for it is much increased in Lambeth, & in Wandsworth (as I told you) from whence People rather run away. It is to be ascribed rather to the unseasonable Weather that hath beene of late; & most of all to the wise Goodnesse of God, who intends to shew, that wee are not yet so safe as sucure Sinners imagin. I observe that Peo-

[163]

ple grow remisse already, & their Fervours are already cooled. Wee had nothing *so good a Congregation yesterday as wee used to have*: & therefore God may in mercy quicken us againe to mind our Duty, & rouse up dull Souls by this new Alarm. At least it may have this Effect, to keepe from flocking to the Towne as fast as they may be disposed to; & also continue in Men's Minds a Dread of the Sicknesse, whenever wee mention it, which is so unaccountable. You hope, I see, that I should be able to acquaint you with its *Nature*: but truly, after all my *Inquiries & Observations*, I can *learne little*, But that it *seises upon People strangely, & handles them variously*. Some are *affected* in *one manner, & some another, & some are smitten* that stir *not half so much abroad as I*. But this will be too long a Discourse. I do not heare neither of any of your Acquaintance dead: but I said, I believe, wee shall miss many in the Conclusion; because I heare now & then of some that I knewe that are swept away a good many Weeks ago, before I heard of it. Wee have but a few dead in the Parish this Week, (Thanks be to God for it) though all our neighbouring Parishes have had an Increase &c.

Your most affectionate Friend

S. P.

Dec: 5. [1665].

My Friend,

. . . . . .

Just now came Newes to mee by one that is come from the *Clarks Hall*, that *the Sicknesse is decreased* above *an 100;* which is a great *Mercy;* for we feared an *Increase.* The *just Number* they would not *declare*, because my *L*d. *Mayor* must have *it first*: & I heard lately that he *imprisoned* one of the *Officers*, because they *spread Abroad the Account, before* they *came to him*: which indeed was *unhandsome.* There was *not one* dyed at *Westminster* on *Sunday* last; which is a Thing seldome happens in healthfull Times.

Farewell.

[*S. P.*]

[164]

December 14. [1665].

My Friend,

I cannot send you so good Newes as I did the last Week of the *Decrease* of the Sicknesse. . . . It is not much indeed: but it's something sad at this Time of the Yeare, not to see it still fall more & more. So wee promised ourselves that it would; & many are returned upon that Presumption. But wee must all look up to an higher Hand, who still thinks good to hold his Rod over us, & who alters the Weather as he pleases; on which depends very much, I persuade myself, these Ebbs & Flows of this Disease. If it do not leave us this Winter, God knows when I shall see you: for I suppose you will scarce be persuaded to come to *Clapham*, though you love it so well, if the Citty be not quite clear of it. . . . I have enquired, I assure you, about a *Man* to do my *Buiinesse here sometimes*: but the Towne is empty of all such Persons; & *he that was wont to do it is dead, I am sure; for I buried him;* it being his *Desire*, though he *lived* in *St. Martin's Parish.* I am apt to think sometimes, that none of my Neighbours are so burthened as I: but Use & Custome hath now made it easy, & I forget what it is that I do continually. . . .

[*S. P.*]

Decembr 21. [1665].

The Towne now begins to fill againe. . . . There is a great *Increase of the Sicknesse this Week.* . . .

[*S. P.*]

Decembr 23 [1665].

Wee have *never a one yet dead* of the *Plague* [in our Parish this Week], as it is judged: though 3 of other Diseases. . . .

[*S. P.*]

APPENDIX J

FROM FLAVIUS JOSEPHUS, *Works*, 7TH ED. (1773), VOL. IV, BK. VII, CH. 12.

How easily were these superstitious wretches [*i. e.* the Jews] seduced into a belief of false oracles, counterfeits and impostors! But when they were at any time premonished from the lips of truth itself, by prodigies, and other monitory prognostics of their approaching ruin, they had neither eyes, ears nor understanding to make right use or application of them. As for example now,

What shall we say to the comet that hung over Jerusalem one whole year together, in the figure of a sword?

What shall we think again of that wonderful light that was seen about the altar . . . and continued for the space of half an hour as bright as day. This prodigy was looked upon by the ignorant as a good omen; but it was expounded by those who knew better things, as the forerunner of a war; and the mystery unfolded before it came to pass.

At the same festival [of the Paschal Feast], there was another prodigy of a cow delivered of a lamb in the middle of the temple, as they were leading her up to the altar for sacrifice.

The eastern gate of the inner temple was made of solid brass; and so very heavy that it was as much as twenty men could do every night to shut it: besides that it was fastened with iron bolts and bars, mortissed into a huge threshold of one entire stone. This gate, about the sixth hour of the night, opened of itself: and . . . the wiser sort . . . foretold desolation to the city.

Some short time after the festival was over, . . . there appeared a prodigy of a vision so extraordinary, that I should hardly venture to report it, if I could not produce several eye-witnesses that are yet living to confirm the truth of it; and if the calamities that were foretold, had not come to pass. There were seen up and down in the air, before sun-set, chariots and armed men all over the country, passing along with the clouds round about the city.

Upon the feast of Pentecost, as the priests were a-going to officiate, . . . they heard at first a kind of confused murmur; and after that, a voice calling out earnestly in articulate words, *Let us be gone, let us be gone.*

But I come now to a story that passes all the rest. A matter of four years before the war [with Titus], when the city was in a profound peace, and flowing in plenty, there was one Jesus the son of Ananus, a plain country fellow, who coming to the feast of Tabernacles . . . brake out on a sudden into this exclamation over and over. "A voice from the east, a voice from the west; a voice from the four quarters of the world; a voice to Jerusalem, and a voice to the temple; a voice to new married men and women; and a voice to the whole nation." This was his cry day and night, from place to place, through every street of the city. Some great men in the government took such great offence at so ill boding a liberty, that they ordered the man to be taken up and severely whipt. He took the punishment without returning so much as one word, either by the by, or in his own defence, or to complain of hard measure; but still he went on and on with the same things over and over again, calling and denouncing as before. The magistrates began now to inspect (as they had reason for it) somewhat of a divine impulse in what he said; and that he spake by an extraordinary spirit. He was carried, upon this, to Albinus the governor of Judaea; who caused him to be lashed to the very bones, which he took without either tears or supplication; only in a mournful voice, as well as he could, he followed every stroke with a *Wo, wo to Jerusalem!* Albinus, as his judge, fell then to asking him what he was, whence he came, where he was born, and what he meant by that way of proceeding? But he gave him no answer. This was his way all along, till Albinus was fain to discharge him at last as a madman. From that time to the beginning of the war, he was never known to visit or speak to any of the citizens; or to make use of any other than that doleful form of words, *Wo, wo to Jerusalem!* He never gave an ill word to those that daily scourged him, or a good one even to those that fed him: but his answer was to all people alike, an ominous presage. He was observed to be still more clamorous upon festivals, than upon other days: at this rate he went on for seven years and five months; and neither his voice nor his strength failing him, till the seige of Jerusalem verified his predictions. After this he took the tour of the wall once again, crying out, with a stronger voice than ordinary, *Wo, wo to this city, this temple, and this people!* concluding at last with a *Wo, wo be to myself!* And in this instant he was taken off with a stone from an engine in the middle of all his forebodings.

APPENDIX K.

From the Bills of Mortality.
General Bills of the Plague in London and Suburbs from 1603 to 1666.[2]

Year	Plague	Year	Plague
1603	33,417	1635	0
1604	896	1636	10,400
1605	444	1637	3,082
1606	2,124	1638	363
1607	2,352	1639	314
1608	2,262	1640	1,450
1609	4,240	1641	1,375
1610	1,803	1642	1,274
1611	627	1643	996
1612	64	1644	1,492
1613	16	1645	1,871
1614	22	1646	2,365
1615	37	1647	3,597
1616	9	1648	611
1617	6	1649	67
1618	18	1650	15
1619	9	1651	23
1620	2	1652	16
1621	11	1653	6
1622	16	1654	16
1623	17	1655	9
1624	0	1656	6
1625	35,417	1657	4
1626	634	1658	14
1627	4	1659	36
1628	3	1660	13
1629	0	1661	20
1630	1,317	1662	15

[2] The only Bills before 1603 are for 1592 (Mch.-Dec.) when 11,503 died of the Plague.

1631............	274	1663............	12
1632............	8	1664............	5
1633............	0	*1665............	68,596
1634............	1	†1666............	1,998

* Dec. 20, 1664 to Dec. 19, 1665.

† Dec. 20, 1665 to Dec. 19, 1666.

The Weekly Bills of Mortality in London and Suburbs from 20 *Dec.,* 1664 *to* 19 *Dec.,* 1665.

Week ending	97 Parishes within the Walls. Ttl.	Pl.	16 Parishes Without. Ttl.	Pl.	12 Out-Parishes of Mid. & Surrey. Ttl.	Pl.	5 Westm. Parishes. Ttl.	Pl.
Dec. 27, 1664	60	0	125	0	67	1	39	0
Jan. 3, 1665	66	0	136	0	102	0	45	0
Jan. 10, 1665	95	0	142	0	100	0	57	0
Jan. 17, 1665	90	0	154	0	113	0	58	0
Jan. 24, 1665	104	0	184	0	118	0	68	0
Jan. 31, 1665	88	0	143	0	115	0	63	0
Feb. 7, 1665	80	0	150	0	99	0	64	0
Feb. 14, 1665	85	0	180	0	121	1	76	0
Feb. 21, 1665	82	0	158	0	89	0	64	0
Feb. 28, 1665	67	0	156	0	106	0	67	0
Mch. 7, 1665	83	0	176	0	165	0	77	0
Mch. 14, 1665	72	0	197	0	105	0	59	0
Mch. 21, 1665	69	0	133	0	98	0	63	0
Mch. 28, 1665	68	0	160	0	74	0	51	0
Apr. 4, 1665	74	0	138	0	86	0	46	0
Apr. 11, 1665	81	0	149	0	107	0	45	0
Apr. 18, 1665	66	0	126	0	93	0	59	0
Apr. 25, 1665	65	0	145	0	119	0	69	0
May 2, 1665	70	0	125	0	127	0	66	0
May 9, 1665	54	1	123	1	114	1	56	4
May 16, 1665	55	0	126	0	116	1	56	2

[170]

May	23,	1665	63	0	125	2	129	7	63	5
May	30,	1665	56	0	127	4	145	9	72	4
June	6,	1665	69	0	135	10	138	32	63	1
June	13,	1665	67	4	179	27	238	71	74	10
June	20,	1665	64	10	192	34	258	105	101	19
June	27,	1665	49	4	225	55	291	153	119	55
July	4,	1665	93	23	360	166	345	176	208	105
July	11,	1665	86	28	473	251	455	286	254	160
July	18,	1665	141	56	735	416	595	417	290	200
July	25,	1665	241	128	1210	755	857	628	477	332
Aug.	1,	1665	228	111	1539	990	804	587	443	322
Aug.	8,	1665	341	208	1992	1280	1105	879	592	450
Aug.	15,	1665	496	304	2747	1924	1404	1119	672	533
Aug.	22,	1665	538	366	2861	2139	1571	1244	598	488
Aug.	29,	1665	933	700	3627	2928	2045	1759	891	715
Sept.	5,	1665	1118	864	3736	3151	2549	2261	849	712
Sept.	12,	1665	1154	896	3488	2936	2250	2030	798	681
Sept.	19,	1665	1493	1189	3631	3070	2258	2091	915	815
Sept.	26,	1665	1268	1025	2688	2252	1794	1643	710	613
Oct.	3,	1665	1149	948	2258	1922	1623	1469	690	590
Oct.	10,	1665	1109	916	1850	1570	1512	1340	597	501
Oct.	17,	1665	774	646	1150	929	835	791	360	299
Oct.	24,	1665	392	295	603	456	601	498	210	172
Oct.	31,	1665	325	233	470	356	435	323	158	119
Nov.	7,	1665	418	314	546	445	609	488	214	167
Nov.	14,	1665	346	262	397	209	460	376	156	103
Nov.	21,	1665	195	127	298	217	302	235	110	73
Nov.	28,	1665	136	82	156	82	178	125	74	44
Dec.	5,	1665	71	24	139	64	160	90	58	32
Dec.	12,	1665	94	57	132	70	147	74	69	42
Dec.	19,	1665	126	66	156	75	187	106	56	34

APPENDIX L.

A general Bill of Mortality by Parishes for the Year ending Dec. 19, 1665.
From Bell's *London's Remembrancer.*
The 97 Parishes within the Walls.

	Total Burials	Plague
St. Albans Woodstreet	200	121
St. Alhollowes Barking	514	330
St. Alhollowes Breadstreet	35	16
St. Alhollowes the Great	455	426
St. Alhollowes Hony-lane	10	5
St. Alhollowes the Lesse	239	175
St. Alhollowes Lumbardstr.	90	62
St. Alhollowes Staining	185	112
St. Alhollowes the Wall	500	356
St. Alphage	271	115
St. Andrew Hubbard	71	25
St. Andrew Vndershaft	274	189
St. Andrew Wardrobe	476	308
St. Aldersgate	282	197
St. Anne Black-Friars	652	467
St. Antholins Parish	58	33
St. Austins Parish	43	20
St. Barthol. Exchange	73	51
St. Bennet Fynch	47	22
St. Bennet Gracechurch	57	41
St. Bennet Pauls Wharf	355	172
St. Bennet Sherehog	11	1
St. Botolph Billingsgate	83	50
Christs Church	653	467
St. Christophers	60	47
St. Clements Eastcheap	38	20
St. Dionis Back-church	78	27

	Total Burials	Plague
St. Dunstans East	265	150
St. Edmunds Lumbard	70	30
St. Ethelborough	195	106
St. Faiths	104	70
St. Fosters	144	105
St. Gabriel Fenchurch	69	39
St. George Botolphlane	41	27
St. Gregories by Pauls	376	232
St. Hellens	108	75
St. James Dukes place	262	190
St. James Garlickhithe	189	118
St. John Baptist	138	83
St. John Evangelist	9	0
St. John Zacharie	85	54
St. Katherine Coleman-streete	299	213
St. Katherine Creech	335	231
St. Lawrence Iewry	94	48
St. Lawrence Pountney	214	140
St. Leonard Eastcheap	42	27
St. Leonard Fosterlane	335	255
St. Magnus Parish	103	60
St. Margaret Lothbury	100	66
St. Margaret Moses	38	25
St. Margaret Newfishst.	114	66
St. Margaret Pattons	49	24
St. Mary Abchurch	99	54
St. Mary Aldermanbury	181	109
St. Mary Aldermary	105	75
St. Mary le Bow	64	36
St. Mary Bothow	55	30
St. Mary Colechurch	17	6
St. Mary Hill	94	64
St. Mary Mounthaw	56	37
St. Mary Summerset	342	262
St. Mary Stayning	47	27
St. Mary Woolchurch	65	33

	Total Burials	Plague
St. Mary Woolnoth	75	38
St. Martins Ironmonger	21	11
St. Martins Ludgate	196	128
St. Martins Orgars	110	71
St. Martins Outwich	60	34
St. Martins Vintrey	417	349
St. Matthew Fridaystreet	24	6
St. Maudlins Milkstreet	44	22
St. Maudlins Oldfishstreet	176	121
St. Michael Bassishaw	253	164
St. Michael Cornhill	104	52
St. Michael Crookedlane	179	133
St. Michael Queenhith	203	122
St. Michael Queene	44	18
St. Michael Royall	152	116
St. Michael Woodstreet	122	62
St. Mildred Breadstreet	59	26
St. Mildred Poultrey	68	46
St. Nicholas Acons	46	28
St. Nicholas Coleabby	125	91
St. Nicholas Olave	90	62
St. Olaves Hartstreet	237	160
St. Olaves Iewry	54	32
St. Olaves Silverstreete	250	132
St. Pancras Soperlane	30	15
St. Peters Cheaps	61	35
St. Peters Cornhill	136	76
St. Peters Pauls Wharfe	114	86
St. Peters Poore	79	47
St. Stevens Colmanstr.	560	391
St. Stevens Walbrooke	34	17
St. Swithins	93	56
St. Thomas Apostle	163	110
Trinitie Parish	115	79
Buried in the 97 Parishes within the walls.	15,207	
Whereof of the Plague	9,887	

The 16 *Parishes without the Walls.*

	Total Burials	Plague
St. Andrew Holborne	3958	3103
St. Bartholomew Great	493	344
St. Bartholomew Lesse	193	139
St. Bridget	2111	1407
Bridewell Precinct	230	179
St. Botolph Aldersgate	997	755
St. Botolph Aldgate	4926	4051
St. Botolph Bishopsgate	3464	2500
St. Dunstans West	958	665
St. George Southwark	1613	1260
St. Giles Cripplegate	8069	4838
St. Olaves Southwark	4793	2785
St. Saviours Southwark	4235	3446
St. Sepulchres Parish	4509	2746
St. Thomas Southwark	475	371
Trinity Minories	168	123
At the Pesthouse	159	156

Buried in the 16 Parishes without the Walls, 41,851
Whereof of the Plague 28,888

The 12 *Out-Parishes in Middlesex and Surrey.*

St. Giles in the Fields	4457	3216
Hackney Parish	232	132
St. James Clarkenwell	1863	1377
St. Katherines Tower	956	601
Lamberth Parish	798	537
St. Leonards Shoreditch	2669	1949
St. Magdalen Bermondsey	1943	1362
St. Mary Newington	1272	1004
St. Mary Islington	696	593
St. Mary Whitechappel	4766	3855
Redriffe Parish	304	210
Stepney Parish	8598	6583

	Total Burials	Plague
Buried in the 12 Out-Parishes of Middlesex and Surrey	28,554	
Whereof of the Plague		21,420

The 5 Parishes in Westminster.

St. Clement Danes	1969	1319
St. Paul Covent Garden	408	261
St. Martins in the Fields	4804	2883
St. Mary Savoy	303	198
St. Margaret Westm.	4710	3742

Whereof at the Pesthouse	156	
Buried in the five Parishes of Westminster,	12,194	
Whereof of the the Plague		68,596

The total of all the Christenings for the year	9,967
The total of all the Burials	97,306
Whereof, of the Plague	68,596

BIBLIOGRAPHY[3]

BELL, JOHN

London's Remembrancer: Or, A true Accompt of every particular Weeks Christenings and Mortality in all the Years of Pestilence within the Cognizance of the Bills of Mortality Being XVIII Years. Taken out of the Register of the Company of Parish Clerks of London, &c. Together with Several Observations on the said Years, and some of their Precedent and Subsequent Years. Published for General satisfaction, and for prevention of false Papers. By John Bell Clerk to the said Company. 1665.

BÈZE, THEODORE DE

A shorte learned and pithie Treatize of the Plague, where in are handled these two questions: The one, whether the Plague bee infectious or no: The other, whether and howe farre it may of Christians bee shunned by going aside. A discourse very necessary for this our tyne, and country; to satisfie the doubtful consciences of a great number. Written in Latin by the famous & worthy diuine Theodore Beza Vezelien; and newly turned into English, by John Stockwood, Schoolmaister of Tunbridge. B. L., 1580. (There is also a Latin ed. of this book, 1636, and another English ed. 1665.)

BOGHURST, WILLIAM, M. D.

Loimographia. An Account of the Great Plague of London in the Year 1665. Now first printed from the British Museum Sloane MS. 349 for the Epidemiological Society. Edited by Joseph Frank Payne, M. D. Late President of the Society. 1894.

BROOKES, RICHARD, M. D.

A History of the most Remarkable Pestilential Distempers that have appeared in Europe for Three Hundred Years last past; with what proved Successful or Hurtful in their Cure, etc. 1721.

[3] No claim is here made of an exhaustive bibliography of Plague literature, but only those titles of leading importance which were accessible to Defoe are included. As already pointed out, Boghurst's "Loimographia" was unknown to Defoe.

BROWNE, JOSEPH

A practical Treatise of the Plague and all Pestilential Infections that have happened in this Island for the last Century, etc. 1720.

CADE, JAMES

Londons Disease and Remedy, or a short and plain Discourse pointing at some probable causes of this present Judgement that lyes upon us together with the most effectual way and means for the removal of it. By Ja. Cade B. D. Rector of St. Andrew Wardrobe, London. 1665.

CHICOYNEAU, FRANCOIS

Relation de la Peste Marseille, donneé par MM. Chicoyneau, Verny et Soullier. Genève: 1721. (An English translation in London the same year. See also Maurice de Toulon.)

COCK, THOMAS

Hygiene, or, a Plain and Practical Discourse upon the first of the six Non-Naturals, viz, Air, etc. 1665.

COLBATCH, SIR JOHN

A Scheme for Proper Methods to be taken should it please God to visit us with the Plague. 1721.

DIEMERBROICK, ISBRANDUS

Tractatus de Peste. Arnheim: 1646. 2nd ed. Amsterdam: 1665. Extracts from this highly important work were translated into English and printed in London in 1666 under the title of "Several Choice Histories [i. e. Cases] of the Medicines Manner and Method in the Cure of the Plague," etc.

DIRECTIONS for the Cure of the Plague as for Preventing the Infection, etc., set down by the College of Physicians. By the Kings Majesties Special Command. May, 1665.

DIRECTIONS for the Prevention and Cure of the Plague Fitted for the Poorer sort. 1665.

DISTINCT NOTES of the Plague. By the Explainer. 1722. (This was written in answer to "Some Remarks on three Treatises of the Plague," etc., *q. v.*)

FEATLY, JOHN

A Divine Antidote against the Plague; or Mourning Tears, in Soliliquies and Prayers: As 1. For this General Visitation. 2. For those whose houses are shut up of the Plague. 3. For those who have Risings and Swellings. 4. For those marked with the Tokens. Necessary for all Families as well in the Country as in the City, in the time of Pestilence. By John Featly, Chaplain to His late Majesty [Charles I]. 1665.

GADBURY, JOHN

Londons Deliverance Praedicted; in a Short Discourse on Plagues in General. August 1665.

GARENCIÈRES, THEOPHILUS, DR.

A Mite cast into the Treasury of the City of London: A Discourse on the Plague. 1665.

GOLGOTHA; or, a Looking-Glass for London, and the Suburbs thereof. Shewing the Causes, Nature and Efficacy of the present Plague, and the most hopeful Way for Healing. With an humble Witness against the Cruel Advice and Practice of Shutting up unto Oppression. Both now and formerly experienced to increase, rather then prevent the spreading thereof. By J. V. grieved for the Poor, who perish daily hereby. London, Printed for the Author, Anno, 1665.

GRAUNT, JOHN

Reflections on the Weekly Bills of Mortality, for the Cities of London and Westminster, and the Places adjacent: But more especially, so far as they relate to the Plague, and other Mortal Diseases that we English-men are most subject to. With an Exact Account of the greatest Plagues that ever happened since the Creation; and of the Weekly Bills of the four great Plagues in London, compared with those of this present year. 1665.

HARVEY, GIDEON, M. D.

A Discourse of the Plague, etc. 1665.

HODGES, NATHANIEL, M. D.

Loimologia, sive Pestis nuperae apud Populum Londinensem grassantis narratio. 1672. (Translated into English by Dr. John Quincy, 1720.)

An Account of the Rise, Progress, Symptoms and Cure of the Plague, being the substance of a Letter from Doctor Hodges to a Person of Quality. May, 1666. (Whether or not this letter was printed the same year it was written, I am not sure. It appears, however, in "A Collection of very valuable and scarce Pieces," etc., 1721. Ed.)

KEMP, W.

A Brief Treatise of the Nature, Causes, Signes, Preservation from, and Cure of the Pestilence. Collected by W. Kemp, Mr. of Arts, MDCLXV.

LONDON'S DREADFUL VISITATION: Or, a Collection of all the Bills of Mortality for this Present Year: Beginning the 27th. [an error for the 20th.] of December 1664. and ending 19th. of December following: As also, The General or whole years Bill: According to the Report made to the King's Most Excellent Majesty, By the Company of Parish Clerks of London, &c. 1665.

MASSA, N.

Liber N. Massae de Peste Contractus. 1721.

MAURICE DE TOULON.

Traite de la Peste. Genève: 1721. (Accounts of the Plague at Naples, Marseilles, etc.)

MEAD, RICHARD, M. D.

A Short Discourse concerning Pestilential Contagion, and the Methods to be used to prevent it. 1720. (This book went through six editions before the close of 1720, a 7th ed. in 1721, an 8th in 1722, and a 9th in 1744.)

DOCTOR MEAD'S Discourse explain'd. 1722.

PATRICK, SIMON

A Brief Exhortation to those who are shut up from our Society, and deprived at present of Public Instruction. 1665.

A Consolatory Discourse, perswading to a chearful Trust in God in these Times of trouble and danger. By Simon Patrick, Rector of St. Pauls Covent Garden. 1665.

POORE MANS IEWELL, The

that is to say, a Treatise of the Pestilence. Vnto the which is annexed a declaration of the vertues of the hearbes *Carduus Benedictus,* and Angelica: which are verie medicinable, both against the Plague, and also against many other diseases. Gathered out of the books of diuers learned Physitions. Imprinted at London for George Byshop, Anno 1579.

PYE, GEORGE, M. D.

A Discourse of the Plague; wherein Dr. Mead's Notions are . . . refuted. 1721.

QUINCY, JOHN, M. D.

An Essay on the Different Causes of Pestilential Diseases, and how they became Contagious. With Remarks upon the Infection now in France. 1720. 3rd ed. 1721.

SHUTTING UP OF INFECTED HOUSES, The

as it is practised in England, soberly debated. 1665.

SOME OBSERVATION on the Plague, etc. 1721.

SOME REMARKS on three Treatises of the Plague, viz.

1. Dr. Meads' Short Discourse; 2. Dr. Mead's Short Discourse Explain'd; 3. Dr. Pye's Discourse of the Plague. 1721, 1722.

SYDENHAM, THOMAS, M. D.

Febris pestilentialis et pestis annorum 1665-6.

Observationes Medicae circa Morborum acutorum historiam et curationem. 1676.

THOMSON, GEORGE

Loimotomia, or the Pest Anatomized. 1666.

THUCYDIDES

The Plague of Athens, which happened in the second year of the Peloppennesian Warre, first described in Greek by Thucydides, then in Latin by Lucretius. Now attempted in English by Tho Sprat, (An excellent Piece) Sold by Henry Brome at the Gun in Ivy Lane. 1665.

VINCENT, THOMAS

God's Terrible Voice in the City: wherein you have

I. The sound of the Voice, in the Narration of the Two late Dreadful Judgments of Plague and Fire, inflicted by the Lord upon the City of London; the former in the Year 1665, the latter in the Year 1666. II. The Interpretation of the Voice, in a Discovery, 1. of the Cause of these Judgments, where you have a Catalogue of Londons sins. 2. Of the Design of these Judgments, where you have an enumeration of the Duties God calls for by this Terrible Voice. Printed in the Year 1667.

WILLIS, THOMAS, M. D.

A plain and easie Method for preserving those that are well from the infection of the Plague . . . and for curing such as are infected with it. 1691. (Written in 1666.)

De Febribus, etc., 1659.

DATE DUE